For Andrea

TABLE OF CONTENTS

Introduction 1

PART I, BIG CITIES

Atlanta, Georgia 5
Austin, Texas 15
Boston, Massachusetts 27
Chicago, Illinois 37
Los Angeles, California 51
Minneapolis, Minnesota 65
New Orleans, Louisiana 75
New York, New York 87
San Francisco, California 101
Seattle, Washington 115
Washington, D.C. 127

PART II, SMALLER TOWNS AND RESORTS

Boulder, Colorado 141
Northampton, Massachusetts 153
Palm Springs, California 163
Port Townsend, Washington 173
Provincetown, Massachusetts 183
Santa Fe, New Mexico 193
Tucson, Arizona 205

Index 217

INTRODUCTION

When I began this project, I was thrilled with the idea of putting all of the lesbian-owned Bed & Breakfasts, restaurants, bookstores and coffeehouses I had ever come across into one collection — and writing a commentary about every single one of them. It had never been done before. My original intention, then, was to list only lesbian-owned places, and make this a truly lesbian travel guide. And I was determined to never let your best interests slip from my mind: where to find all of the wonderful women.

It quickly dawned on me that the lesbian travel industry is still in its infancy. A B&B here, a restaurant there — only a few American cities can boast competition between lesbian-owned businesses, such as Provincetown, Santa Fe and Northampton. And while our job as tourists is to revel 24 hours a day in being lesbian, clearly, somebody needs to cater to us.

The goal, then, became to write an all-in-one lesbian travel book, with sightseeing recommendations, lesbian friendly restaurants and hotels, and general information about when to go, how to get there, and who to call once you arrive; a guide that focuses on how to tap into the lesbian community in cities across America. Say, for example, that you have a trade show to attend in New Orleans, and want a place to escape from your co-workers after hours. Or maybe you're visiting Austin, Texas with your girlfriend and want to hear some local music. Where do you go? And, more importantly, will there be any lesbians once you get there? Needless to say, if a lesbian-owned business was to be found, it's listed. If not, something else that is lesbian friendly is in its place. Hey, we need to sleep and eat somewhere.

In your travels, you will find that many lesbian hangouts are away from a downtown area. But that is one of the greatest things about being in cahoots with our own people. Traditional "vacation destinations" — areas that have high concentrations of museums, beaches, wilderness areas, historical sites and shopping — are different for the lesbian community. Instead, we enter into ethnically diverse neighborhoods, artist colonies, university towns, and, often, rural settings — places that are often off the beaten path, but are still rich in exploration, and, of course, women.

I've intentionally left out e-mail addresses and URLs in the hopes of discouraging anybody to become an accidental cyber-babe tourist. There is nothing worse than getting somewhere and discovering that the element of surprise is gone because you went surfing too long. As a planning tool, though, I've included a few useful Internet addresses in the "Resources" and "Media" sections of each city's listings. This way, you can find out about concerts, readings and general lesbian gay-la before your arrival. And be sure to check out the Weather Channel's Web page before every trip, at www.weather.com.

Finally, remember that things constantly change. What was once your favorite night club may not be there the next time you visit. For that reason, I have made every effort to include the most up-to-date information, but please call ahead just in case.

So, leave your computer behind, board that airplane, and whoop it up in the company of women!

— *Lori Hobkirk*

PART 1

Big Cities

Atlanta, Georgia

area code 404

WHAT TO EXPECT

All of the rumors of Atlanta being a hip city in a conservative corner of the U.S. are true. Baby boomers have infiltrated the Midtown neighborhoods — Virginia-Highland and Morningside, in particular. Young blood has created funky hangouts, charming restaurants and a spirit that is so charged, people can hear its hum throughout the South. Thankfully, a large lesbian community thrives here, and, unlike other cities, hasn't been shooed to the outskirts of town.

But Atlanta is quickly becoming the Los Angeles of the South. People spend way too much time in their cars, and tourists are doomed without one because things are spread out. It's not unusual, for example, to find yourself in a traffic jam on a tiny street when all you wanted to do was take a short cut through a seemingly quiet neighborhood. And there are no bike lanes whatsoever. So, what's a woman to do?

Relax. Once you learn the major corridors, getting around is easy. At all costs, though, avoid what's known as "Malfunction Junction," the intersection of Interstates 85 and 285. Also, ignore all of the 34 different Peachtree streets and avenues; it's mind boggling and enough to drive a tourist batty. Imagine suddenly finding yourself at the corner of West Peachtree Street and Peachtree Street Northeast. Huh? What were city planners thinking? But just in case you accidentally end up there, it might be wise to pack a global positioning system unit in your fanny pack before leaving home.

Never fear, though. In Atlanta's lesbian circles there are only three

GAY USA

Lori Hobkirk

major "dyke drives" to be concerned with: Piedmont, North Highland and McClendon. Both Piedmont and Highland are major north-south thoroughfares through the gay- and lesbian-populated neighborhoods of Ansley, Virginia-Highland and Morningside.

Stretching from North Avenue to Rock Springs Road, Highland boasts cute shops, cafes, used book stores, unique clothing shops and galleries. Even the fire department's refurbished exterior at the Virginia-Highland intersection fits in with the local sentiments by sporting cute red-and-white-striped awnings, and red benches along the sidewalk. And eclectic eateries and galleries are constantly popping up in the Morningside area.

In the spirited Little Five Points part of town, McClendon Avenue begins at Moreland Avenue and the Charis women's bookstore, and heads east toward the Flying Biscuit Cafe — an establishment that many lesbians consider the epicenter of Atlanta's dyke community. Not only does it live up to its namesake of baking heavenly biscuits — there is a wall sculpture above the bar of a gilded angel carrying a tray of the fluffy demons — but it is co-owned by three lesbians, one of them being Emily Saliers of the Indigo Girls. Needless to say, the place attracts women like gravy to biscuits. A lesbian's trip to Atlanta would be incomplete without eating there a few times.

What To Bring

Atlanta can be hot and humid. Therefore, cotton is in order. Jeans and a short-sleeved cotton shirt are acceptable dinner wear. A straw hat or baseball cap is essential for keeping out the afternoon rays. And you absolutely must pack a swimsuit.

Best Time To Visit

In the spring and fall the weather is usually sunny, warm and flawless, although a weekly downpour — or two or three — can be expected.

Getting Around

Unless you plan on riding the **Metro Atlanta Rapid Transit**

ATLANTA

Authority (848-4711), rent a car. MARTA is reliable, but designed for commuters from the outlying suburbs into the downtown area, not for tourists who want to move from one neighborhood to another.

STAY

Guest Houses

The Bonaventure (650 Bonaventure Ave., 817-7024). A giant, restored house that is warm and cozy, with a fireplace in every room. The gracious hostesses will pick up visitors at the nearby MARTA station upon arrival. Near Ansley, Little Five Points and the Virginia-Highlands areas. Lesbian-owned. $75-105.

SEE-DO

In and Around Atlanta

African-American Panoramic Experience (135 Auburn Ave. NE, 521-2739). African-American museum containing African art by local and national black artists. Located in the Martin Luther King Jr. District.

Atlanta History Center (130 W. Paces Ferry Rd., 814-4000). Showcases the 1928 classic Swan House, the rustic 1840s Tullie Smith Farm, gardens and trails, library, archives and a museum shop. And has a gay and lesbian section, as well.

CNN Studio Tour (Techwood Dr. and Marietta St., 827-2300). Welcome to Ted Turner's life. The 45-minute tour explores the megabusiness of telecommunications, even as studio sessions are being broadcast. Call ahead for reservations. Adults, $6; children $3.50.

Cyclorama (800 Cherokee Ave., 624-1071). An immense painting in-the-round recreating the 1864 Civil War Battle of Atlanta. Completed in 1886 while the wounds were still fresh. The story unfolds as you listen and look from a revolving chair. Adults, $5; children 6-12, $4.

Donna Van Goghs Inc. (1651 McLendon Ave., 370-1003). A funky gallery of functional arts and crafts. Buy some gifts for folks back

GAY USA   Lori Hobkirk

home while waiting in line for a table at the Flying Biscuit Cafe. As they say, it's "art for all y'all."

High Museum of Art (1280 Peachtree St., 733-4400). Atlanta's largest art museum, featuring European and American painting, photography and graphics.

Margaret Mitchell House (999 Peachtree St., 249-7012). Mitchell will probably always have the honor of being known as Atlanta's First Lady, as well as being given an honorary lesbian status by others. The truth is she wrote a really good smutty novel — *Gone with the Wind* — and now we can all visit the apartment where she wrote the bestseller.

Martin Luther King Jr. Historic District (Auburn Avenue between Jackson and Randolph Streets, 524-1956). Also known as "Sweet Auburn." It's a little chilling being in the neighborhood that kindled the spirit of this century's foremost civil rights leader. Places of interest include the birth home of Martin Luther King Jr., Ebenezer Baptist Church where he preached, the King grave site and reflecting pools, and an exhibit hall and gift shop.

World of Coca-Cola Museum (55 Martin Luther King Jr. Drive, 676-5151). More than 1000 artifacts and commercial reruns tracing the century-old history of Coca-Cola using state-of-the-art technology. There is unlimited free Coke at the end of the tour, with sips of Cokes from all over the world throughout the tour. $4.50.

Near Atlanta

Barnsley Gardens (597 Barnsley Gardens Rd., Adairsville, 770/773-7480). Beautiful, well-kept gardens surround 1840's plantation ruins, and feature thousands of daffodils, rhododendrons, roses, water gardens and an herbaceous border.

Chattahoochee Nature Center (9135 Willeo Rd., Roswell, 770/992-2055). Forest and marsh land on the banks of the Chattahoochee River. Has nature and canoe trails, a boardwalk over marshlands, exhibits, activities and seminars for all ages.

Chattahoochee River National Recreation Area (1978 Island Ford Pkwy., 770/952-4419). Rafting the Chattahoochee — or

ATLANTA

"Shooting the 'Hooch" — is a favorite Atlanta pastime. Use the National Park Service rental rafts and shuttle service (770/395-6851) for the best experience. Also, plan on some hiking and mountain biking in the area. It's only a 30-minute drive from Atlanta.

Lane Packing Company (Hwy. 96 E. and Lane Rd., 800/277-3224). Fresh Georgia peaches galore. Pick 'em and eat 'em, pack 'em, or mail 'em home, but take time to sample the fresh peach cobbler and peach ice cream.

KEEP FIT-RECREATION

Frontrunners Atlanta (770/621-5007). Meets Saturday mornings at 8 a.m. in the parking lot behind the Piedmont Park tennis courts.

Women's Outdoor Network (770/479-5773). Conducts frequent outings, such as rock climbing, day hikes, kayaking and canoeing. Call for a schedule.

EAT

Fine Dining

Claudette's French Restaurant (315 W. Ponce de Leon Ave., Decatur, 378-9861). A tasty cafe hidden in a bank building, but well worth the search. Simple food and service that's hard to match. The loyal clientele always votes for Claudette's crème brulée as the best in Atlanta. $15-25.

Indigo Coastal Grill (1397 N. Highland Ave., 876-0676). A restaurant and deli in the Morningside neighborhood. Caribbean atmosphere. Creative chicken and seafood dishes that are on the cutting edge of culinary fashion. Reservations not accepted, so expect a wait. Lesbian friendly. $10-25.

Casual Dining

Crescent Moon (254 W. Ponce de Leon Ave., 377-5623). On the main drag in Decatur, with vegetarian dishes, homemade jams, scratch biscuits, and breakfast until 3 p.m. $3-8.

Dunk 'N Dine (2277 Cheshire Bridge Rd., 636-0197). A comfortable place to relax after a movie, or after the bars close. Typical diner atmosphere. Strong coffee and bright lights. Very gay and lesbian friendly. $2-9.

Flying Biscuit Cafe (1655 McLendon Ave., 687-8888). An extremely popular hangout; the staff is comprised entirely of women. Breakfast is served all day, but don't feel limited to that. There are three types of veggie burgers and four chocolate desserts, including a chocolate chip shake. Try the Bohemian breakfast: a strong cup of coffee and two cigarettes to go. Lesbian-owned. $3-8.

Highland Tap (1026 N. Highland Ave., 875-3673). Loud, dark, basement level — don't let these things turn you away. It's also festive, safe and lesbian friendly. Try the unusual salmon BLT, or the juicy burgers. $3-14.

Murphy's (997 Virginia Ave., 872-0904). An eclectic menu, from honey wheat donuts to seared Atlantic salmon to oat bran waffles. A healthy and satisfying restaurant that's lesbian friendly. $5-14.

Pad Thai (1021 Virginia Ave., 892-2070). The coconut-chicken-lemon grass soup is a regular favorite. Portions are big for the money. Lesbian friendly. $3-15.

Silver Skillet (200 14th St. NW, 874-1388). A classic diner direct from the 1950s — at least by the looks of the wait staff. Macaroni and cheese is listed as a vegetable. But the breakfasts are dynamite. Don't leave Atlanta without tasting the biscuits and gravy, scrambled eggs and cheese grits. $2-6.

Zac's (308 W. Ponce De Leon, 373-9468). A popular gay hangout in Decatur. If it's not raining, the best place to people watch is from a sidewalk table. Try a southern-style pot pie or seafood special. $3-16.

Coffeehouses

Aurora (992 N. Highland Ave., 607-1300). This coffeehouse chain is consistently thought of as the best place for a cup of java in Atlanta.

ATLANTA

The one at the Virginia-Highland intersection is always buzzing with women. $1-5.

Alon's Bakery (1394 N. Highland Ave., 872-6000). A busy neighborhood meeting place in the Morningside area with a nice selection of baked goods. Dog friendly. $1-5.

♫ PLAY-MEET

Dancing

Loretta's (708 Spring St., 874-8125). Caters to the African-American gay and lesbian community with house music and rhythm and blues.

Revolution (1492 Piedmont Ave., 874-8455). Located near the Ansley Mall, look for the rainbow-paneled walls outside. A fairly dressy crowd of trendy, wild gals.

Shahan's Saloon (735 Ralph McGill Blvd., 523-1535). Pool tables, Sunday brunch, mostly lesbians in a bar-type atmosphere.

Girls in the Night (800/970-5833). An all-woman roving dance party that shows up on Friday nights at various locations throughout the city; sexual tension is hot. Pick up a monthly newsletter at Charis Books.

The Otherside (1924 Piedmont Rd., 875-5238). This jeans and T-shirt hangout gets hopping at midnight. Saturday nights, dance to live music on the rain proof patio. Mostly lesbian with some gay men.

💲 SHOP

General Shopping

One of the best places to shop is in the Buckhead Entertainment District — at the intersection of Peachtree Battle and Peachtree Road — which is Atlanta's answer to Beverly Hills. **Lenox Mall** (3393 Peachtree Rd., 233-6767) and **Phipps Plaza** (3500 Peachtree Rd., 262-0992) in Buckhead are Atlanta's two most impressive and expensive shopping places. The **Little Five Points, Candler Park** and the **Virginia-Highlands** areas in midtown are known for bohemian-style shops, coffeehouses and galleries. **Underground Atlanta** (at Alabama and Peachtree Streets) is four city blocks of shops, bars and restaurants literally under the busy downtown streets.

Food Markets

Return to Eden (2335 Cheshire Bridge Rd., 320-3336). Vegetarian supermarket. Shop here for healthful snacks and Chinese medicines, but don't expect deli sandwiches because there aren't any.
Sevananda (1111 Euclid Ave., 681-2831). A natural foods coop in the Little Five Points neighborhood.
Urban Market (752-B N. Highland Ave., 525-7873). A trendy market in the Highland Avenue shopping district. Fresh fruits and grains, sandwiches and drinks.

Pride Shopping

Brush Strokes (1510 Piedmont Ave., 876-6567). A gay gift store in the Ansley Mall. Every kind of paraphernalia imaginable.
Junkman's Daughter (464 Moreland Ave., 577-3188). Clothes, gifts, footwear, smoke shop, tattoos and piercing, and pride stuff, all under one funky roof.

Bookstores

Charis Books and More (1189 Euclid, 524-0304). An extremely popular and sometimes crowded lesbian-feminist bookstore. Nooks and crannies stuffed with literary surprises. CDs, jewelry, cards, pride merchandise and T-shirts.
Outwrite (991 Piedmont at 10th, 607-0082). This has to be the world's prettiest gay and lesbian bookstore, with trendy furniture, hip lighting and a well-planned color scheme.

ATLANTA

Reader's Loft (1402 N. Highland Ave., 881-6511). New Age store in the Morningside area. Books, crystals, incense and Native American art.

🦋 KIDS' STUFF

Sci-Trek Museum (395 Piedmont Ave. NE, 522-5500). Home to more than 100 interactive exhibits. Also offers live demonstrations, workshops, films, overnight parties for children and a museum shop.

Six Flags (7561 Six Flags Rd., 770/948-9290). Southern-style theme park with more than 100 rides, shows and attractions.

Stone Mountain Park (Hwy 78, 770/498-5600). Attractions within the granite-mountain park include a sky lift, ante-bellum plantation, train, paddle wheel riverboat, antique auto and music museum, wildlife trail and Civil War museum. There's also hiking, biking, fishing, swimming and camping to be had.

Wren's Nest (1050 Ralph D. Abernathy Blvd., 753-8535). Visit the home of Joel Chandler Harris, creator of Br'er Rabbit and the Uncle Remus tales. Call for storytelling hours, then listen as Br'er Rabbit and Tar Baby come to life again. Adults, $4; children, $2.

Zoo Atlanta (800 Cherokee Ave. SE, 624-5600). Gorillas, orangutans, black rhinos and elephants, as well as a recreated African rain forest. The zoo is rated among the nation's 10 best.

☼ SPIRITUAL

All Saints MCC (957 N. Highland Ave., 524-9090). In-town church for Atlanta's lesbian and gay community. Sunday morning services at 11 a.m.

Christ Covenant MCC (109 Hibernia Ave., Decatur, 373-2733). Services Sunday at 11 a.m. and 7 p.m.

Circle of Grace Community Church (701 W. Howard Ave., 624-1140). In Decatur, a Christian feminist worshipping community, on Sundays at 6 p.m.

Congregation Bet Haverim (770/642-3467). A Jewish Reconstructionist Synagogue serving the lesbian and gay community.

Goddess Oriented Spirituality Group (770/987-0402).

GAY USA *Lori Hobkirk*

New Age Gays (770/434-7338). Meets weekly to discus spiritual empowerment. For men and women.

RESOURCES

General Information

Welcome South Visitors Center (200 Spring St., 224-2000).
African-American Lesbian and Gay Alliance (770/908-7371).
AIDS Hotline for Women (888-9991).
Feminist Women's Health Center (580 14th St. NW, 874-7551).
Gay and Lesbian Center (71 12th St., 876-5372).
Young Lesbian Art & Craft Exchange (in Decatur, 378-3367).
ZAMI (370-1392). Support-discussion group for African-American lesbians.

Media

Amethyst (373-8750). Gay and lesbian literary journal.

Creative Loafing (688-5623, www.creativeloafing.com). Free Atlanta weekly featuring news and events listings.

Dyke TV. Cable channel 12. Airs Mondays, 9:30 p.m. and Tuesdays, 5:30 p.m.

ETC (888-0063). Weekly gay bar magazine.

Southern Voice (876-1819). The prominent weekly gay and lesbian newspaper.

Still Ain't Satisfied. Music and interviews with a lesbian theme. Airs Mondays, 7-9 p.m. on WRFG, 89.3 FM.

Venus **Magazine** (622-8069). Free monthly magazine for lesbians and gays of color.

Austin, Texas

area code 512

WHAT TO EXPECT

There is an old joke that goes like this: One person asks, "What's in the middle of Texas?" And the other person who has never been to Texas looks perplexed and her eyes focus in deep thought at the ceiling. Then, the person who asked the question knows that the joke was a success and blurts out, "An 'X'!"

Don't ever make the mistake of posing that question to somebody who was born and raised under that "X." Holding both hands to the heart, that person will go into a 30-minute oration about the gently rolling, tree-covered, limestone hills that are sprinkled with spring-fed watering holes — such a voluptuous landscape, so enticing. And she will carry on at length about the people who espouse the spirit of that terrain, who make music and poetry and dance, and who are probably the Muses themselves gathered together, right there in the center of Texas. All right, already!

Anybody who has been to central Texas knows that Austin is that place under the "X." While most of the state is known for its political conservatism, football, and oil and ranching industries, Austin — the state capitol — and the surrounding Hill Country attract a Bohemian crowd: up-and-coming musicians, hippies, world-class scullers, cyclists, and, of course, gays and lesbians. And none of these communities are ghettoized. You are as likely to see a lesbian-frequented restaurant on the north side of town as on the south side. And live music venues are a dime a dozen. In fact, on any given Friday or Saturday night there are about 70 gigs playing around town at nightclubs, restaurants, bookstores, hotel lobbies and coffeehouses.

The Austin music scene is special. It's intimate. It's accessible. And it's very "female." In February 1997, Cris Williamson and Tret Fure did an in-store performance at Austin's women's bookstore Book Woman. Mary-Chapin Carpenter often holds autograph parties at local CD shops. Joan Osborne, while passing through town one night, performed a street concert in the downtown area. And Shawn Colvin, before going on tour, rehearsed her show in front of a hometown audience at the funky Continental Club on South Congress Street — which, by the way, is two blocks from the beautiful, lesbian-owned Park Lane Guest House where you will want to stay.

And, while you are there, you might want to spend more time along South Congress Street. Right now, the area is going through a renaissance. Women, primarily, are buying up old, abandoned warehouses and homes while prices are still affordable. A lesbian couple will be overhauling the old San Jose Motel, across the street from the Continental Club, naming it La Mariposa. The plans include an addition of a restaurant and gallery. Also, there is the wonderful lesbian-owned El Sol y La Luna Latin American restaurant, which is kitty-corner from the Continental Club.

Anywhere you go in or around Awesome, Texas — whether it is South Congress Street, the North Side, or 30 miles away at Travis Lake — as a lesbian, you will feel comfortable. And, more importantly, you will always know what it is that can pull your heart strings when thinking about the middle of Texas.

What To Bring

Short hair, possibly a crew- or buzz-cut, possibly in another color; a cool, cotton dress and work boots, or cotton shorts and a sports bra beneath a tank top. Also, bring deodorant and talcum powder.

Best Time To Visit

Anytime from September through May. The summer's heat and humidity is almost unbearable.

AUSTIN

Getting Around

Rent a car. Things are spread out.

STAY

Hotel

Austin Motel (1220 S. Congress, 441-1157). When the owner inherited the motel, it was old and run-down, but she has since renovated it into a beautiful, charming place. Very lesbian friendly. Suites include Jacuzzi, refrigerator and microwave. $52-112.

Guest Houses

Park Lane Guest House (221 Park Ln., 447-7460). All the buildings on the corner lot have been beautifully remodeled into cheery, livable dwellings. Lesbian-owned. One room in house, $85; three-room cottage that sleeps up to four, $110.

SEE-DO

In and Around Austin

Bats (327-9721). One-and-a-half million Mexican free-tailed bats hang out beneath the Congress Avenue Bridge that crosses Town Lake. From April though October, these bats emerge en masse at dusk.

East Sixth Street (from Congress Ave. to I-35). Austin's heartbeat, this revamped Victorian area has become a miniature New Orleans Bourbon Street. By day it offers boutique and antique shopping, and by night live music is heard through every open door and window.

Elisabeth Ney Museum (304 E. 44th St., 458-2255). Home and studio of one of the state's most prominent sculptors; the beautiful grounds will have you wishing you lived here. Free admission to view the largest collection of her work.

Mount Bonnell Park (Crest of Mt. Bonnell Rd., about one mile past the west end of W. 35th). Austin's highest point, the mountain park's history is haunted by stories of beautiful women jumping to their deaths from the rocky cliffs over the Colorado River, usually because of an insensitive male. Legend has it that if a couple climbs to the summit together they will fall in love, but the third climb with the same person will be fatal.

Mountain Biking. Austin is one of the few cities that can boast inner-city off-road trails, though they are relatively short. Be sure to bring your helmet; those caught without it are slapped with a $50 fine. A few trails of choice: **Barton Creek Greenbelt** is a not-too-tough eight-mile trail; **Bull Creek Greenbelt** is a fun and easy trail with one steep incline; **Forest Ridge Nature Preserve** is so technically challenging that you might want to hike it, but stay clear of the daredevils; **Emma Long Motocross Park** is a very technical, but do-able, four-and-a-half-mile loop; and **McKinney Falls State Park** is twisty, with no major rocks or serious climbs. Cycling maps are on sale at bike shops for $4.95. Or call the **Parks and Recreation Department** (477-PARD). Bicycle rentals are available at **University Schwinn** (2901 N. Lamar, 474-6696), and **Armadillo Sports** (1800 Barton Springs Rd., 478-4128).

Rowing. Town Lake, which is actually a wide spot in the Colorado River, attracts rowers from all over the country for training and competition. To go out on your own, **Austin Rowing Club** (472-0700) operates a boathouse on the lake below the Four Seasons Hotel and offers a 20-hour introductory course throughout the summer. **Texas Rowing** (328-7180) rents boats and offers lessons in single-shell rowing.

Swimming. Austinites brag, and rightly so, about **Barton Springs** (2202-1/2 Barton Springs Rd., 867-3080) whose waters stay at 68 degrees year-round. It has become the city's spiritual center — if you call doing laps with thousands of other Austinites spiritual. The limestone formations of the Hill Country beyond the city have given Central Texas other swimming holes such as **Blue Hole** (847-9127), **Krause Springs** (210/693-4181) and **Hamilton Pool** (264-2740).

Women and Their Work (1710 Lavaca, 477-1064). A gallery showcasing women artists, primarily Texas painters. As a cultural arts organization, Women and Their Work promotes dance concerts, performance art and music. Look for its other presentations around town.

AUSTIN

Zilker Park (2100 Barton Springs Rd., 580-3032). Home to the Taniguchi Oriental Gardens, hike-and-bike trails, and — one of Austin's most cherished treasures — the Barton Springs Pool; the park is the primary open space within city limits.

Near Austin

Caving. Surrounded by a limestone terrain, the Austin area is a hot spelunking destination. Here are a few to visit: **Cascade Caverns** (3 miles south of Boerne, 210/537-4212); **Inner Space Caverns** (I-35 in Georgetown, 863-5545); **Karst Preserve** in southwest Austin has Maple Run Cave and Goat Cave; **Natural Bridge Caverns** (near San Antonio, 210/392-3760); and **Wonder Cave** (near San Marcos, 392-3760).

Enchanted Rock (915/247-3903). The park is dominated by massive, dome-shaped hills of pink granite that are good for rock climbing. Tent camping available for $9 per night.

Travis Lake (473-9437). This 64-mile lake, formed by a dam on the Colorado River, has 17 public parks along its coastline, including the popular, gay-frequented nude beach **MacGregor Park** (266-1644), also known as Hippie Hollow. Leave Austin on FM 2222, then turn left onto RM 620. It's about 15 miles west of Austin.

KEEP FIT-RECREATION

Breakaway Cycling Group (258-1586). A gay and lesbian cycling club.

Frontrunners (473-8334). Meets Sundays, 7:30-8:00 a.m., just west of S. Lamar Boulevard on Riverside Drive. Re-group for brunch and socializing afterward.

EAT

Fine Dining

Carmelo's (504 E. Fifth, 477-7497). Rustic, old Italian atmosphere. The cobbled floors will trick you into thinking that you are in a dark Italian alley. Everything on the menu is delicious, especially the "Red Snapper Mango" — a grilled fillet over a risotto pancake that's dressed with asparagus and a dry vermouth mango sauce. $12-35.

Casual Dining

BB's Mexican Cafe (616 Nueces St., 472-8646). Tucked behind the strip occupied by Star Bar, Coyote Care and Katz's Deli, this barebones nook tends to get lost in the shadows. But there is probably not a better breakfast value around. Austin's trademark breakfast tacos cost about a buck apiece, giving you a scrumptious flour tortilla crammed with eggs and cheese, potatoes, beans, fajita meat, chorizo and guacamole. $2-7.

Castle Hill Cafe (1101 W. Fifth, 476-0728). There is always a line outside this Austin favorite. People wait for hours for crab-lobster enchiladas, spicy Szechuan chicken salad, or jicama-pickled carrot slaw. No reservations except on Valentine's Day. $4-17.

East Side Cafe (2113 Manor Rd., 476-5858). You feel healthier just walking into this funky old house-turned-restaurant. Breezes waft in from the organic garden out back, which produces fresh ingredients for many of the entrees. The mixed field greens salad is a taste of heaven. Frequented by lesbians on the weekends. $3-15.

El Sol y La Luna (1224 S. Congress, 444-7770). The basics in Mexican food — enchiladas, fajitas and flautas — with a Latin-American flair. Try the Plato Cubano: plantains with sour cream on the side, and rice and black beans. Note the Frida Kahlo shrine at the end of the bar. Live Latin American music at night. Lesbian-owned. $3-10.

Guero's Taco Bar (1412 S. Congress, 447-7688). Housed in an old feed and seed warehouse, this is where President Clinton ate when he asked to be taken to Austin's best Mexican restaurant. Eat on the large front porch — it's popular with lesbians. $3-18.

Manuel's Downtown (310 Congress Ave., 472-7555). Plan to spend more than your usual few minutes mulling over the menu, which

AUSTIN

boasts a classic chile relleno en nogada (roasted chile poblano stuffed with pork picadillo, baked, and topped with walnut cream brandy sauce). Happy hour (4-7 p.m.) features half-priced appetizers such as yellow fin tuna ceviche and blue crab nachos. $4-15.

Threadgills (6416 N. Lamar Blvd., 451-5440). As legend goes, this was a gas station in the 1930s until some local guitar pickers set up out front. They drew crowds, the owners started serving beer and food, until, finally, gas was a thing of the past. But the music continues. Now the traditional Southern fare is just as much of a draw: fried chicken, meatloaf and chicken livers. $5-10.

Coffeehouses

Ruta Maya Coffee House (218 W. Fourth St., 472-9638). Home to an eclectic clientele, such as the folks who wander in after a long night on Sixth Street, tarot card readers, and, of course, lesbians. Funky, mismatched tables and reading lamps. Don't be surprised if somebody offers to fluff your aura while you are sitting there. Coffee drinks, $1-3.

Mozart's (3826 Lake Austin Blvd., 447-2900). The deck sticks out over Lake Austin, and mellow jazz and folk music are featured every weekend night. Coffee drinks, $1.50-4.

♪ PLAY-MEET

When Austin's only lesbian bar closed, there were few options left for lesbian night life — as far as bars go. Some of the gay men's bars that cater to women are **Area 52** (474-4849), **'Bout Time** (832-5339) and **Proteus** (472-8922). But remember, this is Austin, one of the music capitals of the world. There is bound to be a hot musical gig happening somewhere. Check out some of these classic venues:

Continental Club (1315 S. Congress, 441-2444). This small club has been on the scene for a long time, attracting a local crowd.

Cactus Cafe (109 N. Sheppard, 255-8127). Nancy Griffith, Lyle Lovett ... you name 'em. If a musician wants to play to a crowd who appreciates music, this is the place.

Austin Music Hall (208 Nueces, 495-9962). Attracts big names and big crowds.

Antone's (2915 Guadalupe, 474-5315). Regular acts include hometown strongwomen Angela Strehli and Marcia Ball.

SHOP

Food Markets

Whole Foods (601 N. Lamar, 476-1206). Since the conglomerate is based in Austin, the downtown store is one of its biggest and best stocked. Natural foods, vitamins, body care products.

General Shopping

South Congress Avenue (between the 1400 and 2000 blocks). The strip south of Town Lake is currently undergoing a face lift. New boutiques are destined to find a home here. Meanwhile, check out some of the mainstays. **Simply Divine** (1606 S. Congress, 444-5546) has all-cotton designer women's and children's clothing. **Electric Ladyland** (1506 S. Congress, 444-2002) — with an emphasis on "electric" — is a flashy vintage clothing shop. **Terra Toys** (1708 S. Congress, 445-4489) sells Earth-sensitive children's pastimes, and has a large children's book section. You would expect a place named **Yard Dog** (1510 S. Congress, 912-1613) to sell lawn ornaments, but it is actually a shop and gallery of Southern folk art, sacred art and visionary art, with a particular fondness for all-things-Elvis. Go figure. The **Herb Bar** (200 W. Mary, 444-6251) is one of Austin's best herbal distributors — and while you're there, pet the neighborhood goat who lives across the street at the green house.

"**The Drag**" (21st to 25th Streets along Guadalupe) is the main shopping area near the University of Texas. There are bookstores, coffee shops, cheap eateries, UT memorabilia gift shops, and a lot of auto and pedestrian traffic.

Sixth Street (between Congress Avenue and I-35). Charming

AUSTIN

restaurants, boutiques and all the live music one can hope to hear.

Music Mania (3909 N. I-35, 451-3361). How can anybody consider visiting Austin without stepping into the Grand Central Station of music stores? This one has made a concerted and courageous effort to welcome the gay and lesbian market.

Bookstores

Book Woman (918 W. 12th, 472-2785). Large and very visible women's bookstore. Carries CDs, cards, T-shirts and queer accessories.

Lobo (3204-A Guadalupe, 454-5406). A gay and lesbian bookstore stocked with periodicals, pride paraphernalia, cards and video rentals.

KIDS' STUFF

Austin Zoo (10807 Rawhide Trail, 288-1490). This privately owned zoo southwest of Austin has a petting corral, a viewing deck, a discovery center, and train and pony rides. Adults, $4; children, $3.

Kiddie Acres (4800 W. Howard Lane, 255-4131). Geared toward families with children 10 and younger, the park features a merry-go-round, Ferris wheel, miniature golf, and boat, car and pony rides.

SPIRITUAL

Dignity Austin (27th and University, 918-1707). Gay and lesbian Catholic Mass and social every second and fourth Saturday at 6 p.m.

Isis Institute for Women's Studies (504 W. 17th St., 474-7669). Classes, retreats and workshops that focus on soul searching, dreams, and finding the goddesses in our lives.

MCC of Austin (708-8002).

Mishpachat Am Echad (452-3852). For Jewish gays, lesbians, partners and friends.

Trinity United Methodist Church (600 E. 50th St., 459-5835).

Unity Austin (2806 Del Curto Rd., 477-7772). Dynamic lesbian minister.

GAY USA   Lori Hobkirk

RESOURCES

General Information

Austin Visitor's Bureau (201 E. Second St., 478-0098).
Austin City Links (www.austinlinks.com). Links to Austin-related news and events, including a page of Austin-area photographs.
Austin Latino Lesbian and Gay Organization (472-2001).
Austin Women's Addiction Referral and Education Center (1524 S. I-35, 326-1222).
Bisexual Network of Austin (370-9573).
Cornerstone Community Center (1117 Red River, 708-1515). Offers meeting rooms and bulletin boards.
Gay and Lesbian Pasta Society (445-5304). Monthly dinners.
Gay and Lesbian Student Association (University of Texas, 458-3971).
Latina Lesbian Organization (472-2001).
SapphFire (323-2476). Lesbian social group that meets the first Friday of each month at the Trinity United Methodist Church (600 E. 50th St.).

Media

Austin Chronicle (454-5766, www.auschron.com). Diverse free weekly covering the Austin music and entertainment scene.
Dyke TV. Cable Channel 10, Tuesdays at 9 p.m.
G-Spot. On KOOP-91.7 F.M., Wednesdays from 2-4 p.m. Features women and drag queens.
Texas Gay and Lesbian Review. Cable Channel 10, Sundays from 11 a.m.-noon.
Texas Triangle (476-0576, www.outline.com/triangle/hp.html). A weekly newspaper covering the San Antonio, Austin and Houston gay and lesbian scene.
The San Antonio Marquise (545-3511). A monthly newspaper covering the Texas gay community in depth, especially the San

AUSTIN

Antonio area.

This Week In Texas (713/527-9111). A free weekly on queer happenings around Houston and Dallas, with some information on Austin.

Festivals

Kerrville Folk Festival (in Kerrville, 210/257-3600). More than 100 bands play original music during the 10-day festival.

Sixth Street Music and Heritage Celebration (478-1704). In August.

Gay and Lesbian International Film Festival (Dobie Theatre, 472-3240). The first two weeks in September.

Acoustic Music Festival (477-9438). Folk, jazz, world beat, blues, rock, Mexican, Central American, Latin American and country musicians perform the third weekend of November.

Boston, Massachusetts

area code 617

WHAT TO EXPECT

People-watching on airplanes can reveal a variety of things about a destination. On flights to Los Angeles or Phoenix, folks don't pack heavy clothing, and they don't take many books because, upon arrival, free time will be spent having fun in the sun. For Boston, however, everyone carries a trench coat, briefcase and satchel of reading material. And before the plane ever leaves the ground, Bostonians tend to bury their noses in ethnographies about ancient civilizations, or engage in highly charged debates about things such as the physics of kite flying, or what kinds of reading material are appropriate for lawyers' waiting rooms. Unless you are accustomed to such heady ritual and have mentally prepared yourself for total immersion in the Land of Educated People, it can all be a bit daunting.

Don't let it get to you, though. Boston is also a lot of fun. The trick is to do everything the guidebooks tell you not to do. Driving, for instance, is often not recommended. Although I wouldn't normally recommend driving in a city that is promoted as a walker's paradise, renting a car is one of the best ways to experience Bostonian culture. And it's exhilarating. The city itself was 300 years old *before* the automobile was invented, and when cars finally *did* make an appearance, Bostonians did not go out of their way to roll out the red carpet. Many of its narrow, winding streets remain exactly that. Just be sure to bring a map with your hotel's location circled.

One outing goal should be Jamaica Pond at the western edge of the lesbian-inhabited Jamaica Plain neighborhood, and part of the famed "Emerald Necklace," a string of parks circling Boston. Jamaica Pond is a popular spot for local women to get some fresh air, walk their dogs, sail, row and fish. And though there is not much more in the area that's of interest to the tourist, it's still worth the stroll down Centre Street, just east of the pond, for some good people watching. Jamaica Plain lesbians have been instrumental in bringing together an ethnically diverse bunch of people, by organizing events at the Jamaica Plain Community Center that are not only for the gay community, but for the entire neighborhood. The rich diversity of Jamaica Plain's people can be seen on Centre Street where there are cafés and coffee shops in which to relax and help you prepare for the drive back downtown.

Once you have returned your rental car and are back on your feet, it's time to visit Cambridge and Harvard Square where there is a distinctively Parisian, Left Bank, intellectual feel. Collegiates read and walk at the same time; bookstores abound; sidewalk cafes overflow into the Squares; and women have impassioned conversations in foreign languages. You'll want to explore this area quite a bit, if not for its international appeal, then for its eclectic character and book shops.

What To Wear

Choose between long, flowing skirts with tights, tight tops and wild hair, or the J. Crew look of woolly sweaters, cotton trousers and crop-top hairdos.

Best Time To Visit

Without a doubt, the Kodak moments take place during the famous New England autumn.

Getting Around

Since **Logan International Airport** (800/235-6426) is near the center of Boston, it is convenient to get downtown by bus or subway. The subway to Cambridge and other outlying neighborhoods can be accessed from the airport, as well as the **Airport Water Shuttle** (330-8680), which will take passengers from the airport's own dock to

BOSTON

Rowes Warf on Atlantic Avenue in downtown. Once you leave the airport, though, Boston's twisty colonial streets take over, and its notoriously reckless drivers conspire to increase your stress level.

STAY

Guest Houses

From $65, including breakfast for two, the **Bed & Breakfast Associates** (449-5302 or 800/347-5088) will find an accommodation for you in Boston by selecting from 400 guest rooms. The drawback is that the place might not necessarily be woman-oriented.

Victorian B&B (536-3285). For women only. Two lesbians in the heart of the gay South End rent an elegant room in their home. $65.

Victorian Townhouse (49 St. Stephen St., 859-9702). Besides its quiet charm, the advantage of staying at this B&B is that it's within walking distance of the Christian Science Center, Copley Square, the subway, the Back Bay, Newbury Street and the South End. An easy walk on the Massachusetts Avenue bridge over the Charles River will take you to Cambridge. Woman-owned. $90-110.

Cambridge Bed and Muffin (576-3166). A reasonable, comfortable and quiet Bed & Breakfast between Harvard, MIT and Boston University. Shared bath. Woman-owned. $60.

Berkeley Residence (40 Berkeley St., 482-8850). Comfortable, affordable guest suites and permanent housing for women. Breakfast included. Affiliated with the YWCA. $38-70.

SEE-DO

In and Around Boston

Women's Heritage Trail (522-2872) Most tourists follow the red bricks of the Freedom Trail through Boston to get a feel for colonialism, but it's pretty much the trail of dead white men. Instead, check out four walking tours that lead through parts of the city's center to learn about how women — both black and white — have contributed to the past four centuries of Boston's history. The "Downtown Walk" focuses on the search for equal rights; the "North End Walk" is about the diversity of cultures; the "South Cove-Chinatown Walk" tells stories of action for social justice (be careful in Chinatown after dark, though. It's also known as the "Combat Zone"); and the "Beacon Hill Walk" introduces women writers, artists and activists. Guidebooks are available via mail, as well as at the **Boston National Park Service Headquarters** (15 State St.), and at **New Words** women's bookstore in Cambridge (186 Hampshire St., 876-5310).

Nichols House (55 Mount Vernon St., 227-6993). The house was the lifelong home of Rose Nichols — noted landscape gardener, suffragette, and protégé of Augustus Saint-Gaudens. This Beacon Hill museum is also headquarters for a spring tour of private local gardens.

Central Square. In Cambridge, midway between Harvard and MIT, the area has become extremely popular with lesbians. It's a good place to babe watch, and the area is littered with coffeehouses and bookstores.

Computer Museum (300 Congress St., 426-2800). A comprehensive exhibit of the history of computer technology, which dates back, oh, about 10 years. Still, it's fascinating to get caught up in it all.

Boston Architectural Center (320 Newbury St., at Hereford St., 536-3170). Always an interesting exhibit, the show might be an homage to an architect's life work, or a collection of neon signs.

Christian Science Church Center (175 Huntington Ave., at Massachusetts Ave., 450-2000). The original Church of Christ, Scientist, founded by Mary Baker Eddy in the late 19th Century, is a work of art. The main attractions are the Mother Church with its Byzantine-like dome, the Publishing Society Mapparium — headquarters of the "Christian Science Monitor" newspaper — and its elegant Sales Room.

Black Heritage Trail (742-5415). Begins in front of the State House at the memorial to the 54th Regiment and leads to 13 sites in the old West End, center of the city's 19th century black community.

Near Boston

Plimoth Plantation (one hour south of Boston on Route 3, take

BOSTON

Exit 4 south and follow signs along the Plimoth Plantation Hwy., 508/746-1622). A "living museum," this re-creation of 17th century Pilgrim life is like being on the movie set of "Pilgrim's Progress."

Orchard House (399 Lexington Rd., in Concord, 369-4118). The home of Louisa May Alcott and her family before she moved to Boston.

Salem Witch Museum (19-1/2 Washington Sq., in Salem, 744-1692). An historically correct, audio-visual recreation of the 1692 witch trials using life-size figures, a sound track and spooky lighting.

KEEP FIT-RECREATION

Chiltern Mountain Club (859-2843). The 1200-member club organizes hikes, bike rides, camping and skiing trips for gays and lesbians in New England.

Ultimate Frisbee Club (661-6378). All lesbian and bisexual women are invited to practice techniques and play in a non-competitive, relaxed atmosphere. Meet on Saturdays between noon and 2 p.m., in Cambridge.

Women Outdoors (364-3266).

EAT

A general rule of thumb is that if a restaurant is in the South End it's going to be fun and on the trendy side.

Fine Dining

Hammersleys Bistro (553 Tremont St., South End, 423-2700). Expensive, dinner-only South End institution. Try the duck confit with caramelized figs. $25-40.

Seasons (In the Regal Bostonian Hotel, Faneuil Hall, 523-4119). Experience Chef Peter's latest menu, inspired by the rhapsody of whatever season it is. Cranberries, crab, corn risotto, camembert tart ... you name it. $10-35.

Casual Dining

Bella Luna (405 Centre St., Jamaica Plain, 524-6060). The funkiest pizzeria in Jamaica Plain. Woman-owned. $5-15.

Blue Wave (142 Berkeley St., 424-6664). Located in the high-energy South End. California-accented food and atmosphere. Wear your hippest clothes. $10-20.

Les Zygomates (129 South St., 542-5108). A taste of Paris in downtown Boston. The atmosphere captures the casual elegance of an authentic French bistro, and the food is equally impressive. Live jazz on Sunday nights. Reservations suggested. $8-20.

Five Seven Five (At the corner of Massachusetts Ave. and Newbury St., 247-9922). A chic, yet casual atmosphere that presents a wide and varied selection of specialties from Asia to Europe, including a sushi bar. A favorite dish is the Thai Lobster served with a coriander basil butter sauce. $8-25.

Centre Street Cafe (597 Centre St., Jamaica Plain, 524-9217). This eclectic neighborhood spot is easily identified by its huge, multi-colored F-O-O-D sign out front. It features vegetarian and vegan fare, with legendary brunches. Very lesbian friendly. $5-15.

Christopher's (1920 Massachusetts Ave., Porter Square, Cambridge, 876-9180). Mexican food, free-range chickens, pastas, local singers and an international beer selection. Gay-owned. $3-12.

Five Seasons (669-A Centre St., 542-9016). An outstanding vegetarian restaurant in Jamaica Plain, but the wait can be ridiculous. Many have compared this place to Greens in San Francisco. Fish is also served. Very lesbian friendly. $7-18.

Mary Chung's (464 Massachusetts Ave., Cambridge, 864-1991). Mandarin-Szechuan hot and spicy food. Lesbian friendly. $5-10.

Union Oyster House (41 Union St., 227-2750). Situated since 1826 in one of the oldest U.S. buildings, this is a Boston tradition. Investigate the "shore dinner," which includes clam chowder, steamers and lobsters, and is served with corn, potatoes and salad. Follow this with a dessert of ginger bread or Indian pudding. $10-30.

BOSTON

Coffeehouses

Cafe Liberty (497-B Massachusetts Ave., Cambridge, 492-9900). These folks are true believers that coffee is a drug: "Drink up and be awake" is their motto. $1-5.

Carberry's (74-76 Prospect St., Cambridge, 576-3530). Groovy coffee hangout. The smell of fresh-baked goods alone makes it worth the visit. $1-6.

Coffee Cantata Bistro and Beans (605 Centre St., Jamaica Plain, 522-2223). One of the neighborhood's favorite night spots, it also offers omelets, ravioli and hand-baked desserts. $3-12.

Toscanini's (899 Main St., Central Square, Cambridge, 491-5877). Perfect for those who want ice cream at 8 a.m., and those who want coffee at midnight.

♫ PLAY-MEET

The Jungle (965 Massachusetts Ave., 427-7807). Friday is Girl Bar; Saturdays is mixed night for gay men and women. The rest of the week it's mixed.

Club Cafe (209 Columbus Ave., South End, 536-0966). The women tend to hang out in the front part of the cafe, while the men seem to congregate in the back. A popular spot for well-dressed women who prefer a decibel level allowing conversation.

Coco's Lazy Lounge and Dance Club (965 Massachusetts Ave., 427-7807). With three tasteful separate spaces, this women's club provides for all possible moods and frequently features local lesbian performers.

Gays for Patsy (446-3115). Country-Western dancing for the gay and lesbian community. On Sunday afternoons, put on your two-stepping shoes and head on out to the **Cambridge Baptist Church** (1151 Massachusetts Ave.) for a gay and lesbian country-western tea dance.

Mercury Bar-Esmé (116 Boylston Place, 482-7799). Sundays are women's nights.

Ryles Jazz Club (212 Hampshire St., Cambridge, 628-0288). Sundays there is a women's tea dance in the afternoon.

GAY USA *Lori Hobkirk*

💲 SHOP

Food Markets

Faneuil Hall Marketplace (Congress St., 338-2323). Once a run-down meeting house, its resurrection has become one of the most popular lunch areas in the city.

Haymarket. Squeezed between Government Center and Faneuil Hall Marketplace, this is where Boston's big open-air food market is held every Friday and Saturday.

Secondhand Stores

Amvets Thrift Store (80 Brighton Ave., Allston, 562-0720). Best prices in Boston on all clothing.

Boomerangs (60 Canal St., 723-2666). More than 5000 square feet of recycled and new clothing, housewares, furnishings and gift ware.

Pride Shopping

Copley Flair (583 Boylston St., 247-3730). Gay-owned department store of gifts and cards.

Clothing

Look for bargains at two giants: **Macy's** (450 Washington St., 357-3000) and **Filene's Basement** (426 Washington St., 357-2100).

Fire Opal (7 Pond St., Jamaica Plain, 524-0262) has the best selection of jewelry, ceramics and clothing, and is woman-owned.

Jet Screamer (1735 Massachusetts Ave., Cambridge, 661-8826). A woman-owned shoes and accessories store.

Newbury Street (in the Back Bay, beginning at Arlington). From the exquisite to the gaudy, the main shopping strip in Boston tends to be on the expensive side. Pick up a "Newbury Street League Map" at information booths at Boston Commons or Boston Public Library.

BOSTON

Harvard Square (at Massachusetts Ave. and John F. Kennedy Dr.). This touristy area features unique shops, bookstores, a variety of cafes and coffee shops, as well as a festive street scene.

Bookstores

Glad Day Books (673 Boylston St., 267-3010). Mostly frequented by men, but there is a good selection of women's titles, as well. Located in the South End.

New Words Bookstore (186 Hampshire St., Cambridge, 876-5310). New England's oldest and largest women's bookstore is located in an unassuming old house, with an assortment of jewelry, CDs, cards, and good lesbian energy.

Globe Corner Bookstore (3 School St., 523-6658). The building dates from 1718 and its fame began when it became a gathering place for 19th Century writers Emerson, Hawthorne, Holmes, Longfellow and Whittier. Now it specializes in travel and adventure books.

KIDS' STUFF

Museum of Science (Science Park, 723-2500). Lots of hands-on scientific and technical exhibits.

New England Aquarium (Central Wharf, 973-5200). A spellbinding undersea world on view along Boston Harbor.

USS Constitution (Charlestown Navy Yard, 426-1812). "Old Ironsides" is the mighty ship that battled the British in 1812.

Boston Tea Party Ship and Museum (Congress Street Bridge, 338-1773). Where kids and adults can get a taste of Revolutionary history.

SPIRITUAL

Am Tivka (493-3105). Jewish gay men and women.

Church of the Covenant (266-7480). Non-denominational lesbian and gay men Christian support group.

Dignity Boston (423-9558). Gay and lesbian Catholics.

Integrity Boston (479-5719). Gay and lesbian Episcopalians.
Metropolitan Community Church of Boston (288-8029). Gay and lesbian Christians.
Women's Spirituality Group (461-5946). Discusses all issues of goddess religions. Meets in Jamaica Plain.

RESOURCES

General information

Boston Visitor's Bureau (536-4100).
Cambridge Women's Center (46 Pleasant St., 354-8807). An ideal place to begin familiarizing yourself with the Boston and Cambridge women's communities.
Bostix (723-5181). Clearinghouse for theater, concert and ballet tickets.
Girlfriends (Fenway Community Health Center, 7 Haviland St., 267-0900 ext. 204). A peer-support group for lesbian and bisexual women of color.
Bisexual Community Resource Center (338-9595).
Gays and Lesbians of Watertown (499-8615). The social group has grown to more than 100 members from Watertown, Newton, Cambridge, Medford and Natick.
Irish-American Gay, Lesbian and Bisexual Group (695-8051). Meets on a regular, informal basis.

Media

Bay Windows (266-6670, www.baywindows.com). Boston's weekly gay and lesbian newspaper.
IN Newsweekly (426-8246). Greater New England's gay, lesbian and bisexual news and entertainment weekly.
Sojourner (524-0415). The best, and only, women's monthly newspaper to turn to for information on local events.

Chicago, Illinois

area codes 312 & 773

WHAT TO EXPECT

Ah, Chicago. In the winter, it is the epitome of all things that are flat and windy; men who wear wool hats with ear flaps are *très chic*; and the words "wind chill" and "Alberta Clipper" are as familiar as long lines outside the Art Institute. In the summer, people escape the hustle-bustle and vacation at northern lakes, that is, if they leave their beloved Lake Michigan at all.

But Chicago carries with it an element of surprise. In the middle of cornfields and soybean crops, nobody expects to find an international city filled with ethnic neighborhoods as rich and abundant as pan pizza and Pad Thai. Who would ever expect to visit Chinatown or Greek Town 1500 miles away from any American ocean? Perhaps, subconsciously, Chicagoans have always considered the city as coastal in its own right, what with its perch along the banks of Lake Michigan, and its miles and miles of sandy beaches and shoreline drives.

And there are more surprises, such as discovering how easy it is to navigate the metropolis's orderly grid of streets, as well as discovering that there is a healthy lesbian subculture in the small Chicago neighborhood of Andersonville, a place not marked on most city maps. At the mention of tiny Swedish neighborhood, most locals get questioning looks on their faces because they have either never heard of the place, or have never been there. Not too many people have a reason to go to Andersonville unless they are female or Scandinavian, or get lost en route from Chicago to the north shore suburbs. And if a woman said she was going to Chicago's gay part of town, the majority of Chicagoland's 8.5 million people would think of Boystown — an alias for the Lakeview area, which lies north of Lincoln Park, and south of Andersonville. But there it is, a four-block strip along North Clark Street between Foster and Bryn Mawr Avenues that is the heart of the lesbian Midwest: Girlstown.

In retrospect, thanks should be given to Edward Brennan for making it easy to find Andersonville. As a frustrated bill collector in the early 1900s, he became tired of chasing all over town for deadbeat tax evaders using streets that changed names every few blocks. So, Brennan designed a grid system that would make more sense. Basically, to get to Andersonville go north along Lake Shore Drive to Foster Avenue, then west about a half mile to Clark Street. There is no major sightseeing to be had in Andersonville except the Swedish Institute, and no upscale hotel, but there are fun shops, with every other one either being owned by a woman or catering to women. And there are several Swedish and Turkish markets to peruse, as well as extremely woman friendly restaurants, and Chicago's premiere women's bookstore — Women and Children First — an anchor of the feminist community. There is also one gorgeous lesbian-owned Bed & Breakfast a few blocks away, Le Ms.

Don't forget that a visit to Chicago must include a day, or three, at one of the many Chicago area beaches on glorious Lake Michigan. In the summer, the majority of Chicago's socializing occurs here. Chicagoans become slaphappy with the chance to be warm and outdoors for three solid, glorious months. Pick up a copy of *The Reader* for a listing of weekly events, and head to the warm sand and fresh water.

What To Bring

In addition to a faux wool ensemble, in the winter be sure to bring a *very* warm coat and pair of boots. Chicago in the summer is hot, sometimes unbearably, so dress accordingly. In the Lakeview-Wrigley area, visit one of the many vintage clothing shops to acquire the local look.

CHICAGO

Best Time To Visit

The best time of year for Chicago has been and forever will be the late spring and early autumn. The first wave of warm weather in May brings a host of fun things from the Chicago International Art Expo and the International Film Festival, to Venetian Night in August — an event for which boat owners gather in Lake Michigan and string lights from mast to stern and bow.

Getting to Andersonville

By car from downtown, take Lake Shore Drive to the Foster exit and go west to Clark Street, which is the third stop light. By bus, take the "No. 22 Clark" that runs between downtown and the Howard Street Terminal, or the "No. 92 Foster" from the Jefferson Park Terminal on Milwaukee Avenue. On the "el," take the Howard-Dan Ryan train (Red Line north-south subway) to the Berwyn "el" stop and transfer to the "No. 92 Foster" bus. Get off at the corner of Clark and Foster.

STAY

Luxury

Inn of Chicago (162 E. Ohio, 800/557-BEST). The best value in the heart of downtown's shopping district, the Magnificent Mile, this hotel is a perennial sponsor of Chicago's annual lesbian and gay international film festival. $129, one bed; $149, two beds.

Guest Houses

Le Ms. (4418 N. Paulina, 773/769-5151). A lesbian-owned Victorian B&B — the only one in Chicago — with three rooms, one of which is an attic apartment with skylights. There is also a library and a baby grand piano in the community room. No kids, no pets, no drugs. It's a ten-minute walk to the Andersonville strip. $60-75.

Magnolia Place B&B (5353 N. Magnolia, 773/334-6860). An Andersonville area Victorian row house with three rooms, fireplaces, brass bed, quilts and wicker furniture. Gay men and lesbians only. $60-70.

Old Town B&B (1451 N. North Park Ave., 312/440-9268). A modern townhouse on a quiet street with antiques, art and a fireplace. Guest rooms have an adjoining library and a luxurious marble bath. Gay-owned, and lesbians are welcome. $75.

SEE-DO

In and Around Chicago

Architecture Foundation River Cruises (312/922-3432). Everybody in Chicago understands and appreciates architecture. There is no reason why you can't as well. Reservations suggested; $18.

Art Institute of Chicago (111 S. Michigan Ave. at Adams St., 312/443-3600). Containing one of the largest impressionist collections in the world, the Art Institute covers every spectrum of art throughout history, from pre-Renaissance oil paintings and Medieval armor to modern art.

Footsteps Theatre (5230 N. Clark, 773/878-4840). Chicago's premier women's theater generally stages four plays from September through June, ranging from an all-woman cast for William Shakespeare's "Taming of the Shrew," to historical vignettes during March's Women's History Month.

John Hancock Center Observatory (875 N. Michigan, 312/751-3681). A 40-second elevator ride takes you to the 94th floor panoramic deck to view Chicago, Lake Michigan and three surrounding states.

Museum of Contemporary Art (220 E. Chicago Ave., 312/280-2660). One of the best collections and presentations of contemporary art in the U.S.

Navy Pier (600 E. Grand, 312/595-7437). The former Navy base has been transformed into a Staten Island-esque fun land with a musical carousel, shops galore, big name stars at the Skyline Stage, and terrific views of the city from the top of the Ferris wheel.

The Field Museum (Roosevelt Rd. at Lake Shore Dr., 312/922-9410). The anthropological world and its people portrayed in more than

CHICAGO

nine acres of natural history exhibitions. Wednesdays are free.

Thousand Waves Spa (1212 W. Belmont, 773/549-0700). For women only. This beautifully renovated, Japanese-inspired spa is the perfect place to relax and rejuvenate. Features steam room, hot tub, sauna, massage and herbal wraps.

Near Chicago

Indiana Dunes State Park (near Chesterton in northern Indiana, 219/926-1952). Forty-five minutes south-east of Chicago on the Indiana shore of Lake Michigan is a 2000 acre park that is a popular summer destination for swimmers, beach bums and dune hikers.

Frank Lloyd Wright Home and Studio (951 Chicago Ave., Oak Park, 708/848-1500). This revolutionary turn-of-the-century home features soaring spaces, colorful art, glass, and bold geometric forms. Tours of other Frank Lloyd Wright homes in Oak Park are available (708/848-1500).

KEEP FIT-RECREATION

Frontrunners (773/267-8756). To walk or run with other women, meet in Lakeview at the Addison Street totem pole, at Lake Shore Drive, every Saturday at 10 a.m., or Tuesday evening at 6:30 p.m.

Tri Women (773/702-6451). A triathlon club for women. Meets regularly for swimming, cycling and running, as well as other activities.

EAT

Fine Dining

Entre Nous (in the Fairmont Hotel, 200 N. Columbus Dr. at Wacker, 312/565-7997). This lite French-American dining room is one of the best deals in the city. You can make a meal out of the appetizers alone: crab cakes, foie gras and smoked salmon. $19-35.

La Donna (5146 N. Clark, 773/561-9400). A very woman-friendly

Italian eatery in the heart of Andersonville. The daily risotto is usually a good bet, as well as the Gnocchi Mona Lisa. Open for lunch and dinner only, with valet parking on weekends. $5-17.

Tomboy (5402 N. Clark, 773/907-0636). An elegant eatery in Andersonville. Selections range from juicy fillet mignon to grilled pork chops to fresh quail. Open for dinner only. Lesbian-owned. $10-20.

Casual Dining

Ann Sathers Restaurant (5207 N. Clark, 773/271-6677). Home style cooking with a definitive Swedish flare. There are two establishments: one in Boystown (Lakeview), the second in Andersonville. Very lesbian friendly. $5-8.

Cafe Selmarie (2327 W. Giddings, 773/989-5595). Located in the Lincoln Square area, this quaint cafe is inconspicuous amid the noisy German beer halls that still dominate the neighborhood. The European-esque bakery sells rum balls the size of softballs. $5-12.

Chicago Diner (3411 N. Halsted, 773/935-6696). This is *the* vegetarian spot in the city. Even Madonna eats here when she's in town. Try the grilled eggplant sandwich. Near the Lakeview area. $5-12.

Cousins (5203 N. Clark, 773/334-4553). The Turkish, health-conscious menu includes a wide variety of freshly made appetizers, lamb and salmon entrees, and homemade desserts. Great selection of Turkish wine, beers and drinks. $3-14.

Ethiopian Village (3462 N. Clark, 773/929-8300). An all-you-can-eat, fork-free, mostly vegetarian buffet for $6.95 is the main attraction at this deep storefront decorated with African art works.

Kopi, A Traveler's Cafe (5317 N. Clark, 773/989-5674). Escape from shopping and enjoy a fine vegetarian lunch, while perusing the cafe's shelves of travel books. $3-7.

Pauline's (1754 W. Balmoral, 773/271-1202). The chairs are a little rickety, but the great omelets make up for that. Fluffy eggs, and blueberry pancakes that could pass as blintzes. Open only for breakfast and lunch. Lesbian friendly. $3-6.

Svea (5236 N. Clark St., 773/334-9619). This sleepy, down-to-earth diner could be the best Swedish discovery since the Vikings found America. Try the Swedish pancakes and lox sandwiches. $3-8.

The Earth Cafe (2570 N. Lincoln, 773/327-8459). In addition to a soulful shopping experience at the attached Healing Earth Resources, the vegetarian cafe leaves you feeling more than satiated. You feel whole again. $4-12.

Coffeehouses

Great Lakes Coffee & Tea (1517 W. Foster, 773/506-1500). Andersonville's intimate coffee shop is around the corner from Clark Street. Features a full espresso bar and desserts.

Halsted Street Cafe (3641 N. Halsted, 773/325-2233). This Lakeview coffee shop sponsors an occasional gay and lesbian open mic night.

Mountain Moving Coffeehouse for Womyn and Children (1650 W. Foster, 773/477-8362). A coffeehouse with entertainment and snacks for women and children. Open most Saturday evenings. Call ahead for program schedules.

Bakeries

A Taste of Heaven (1701 W. Foster, 773/989-0151). Homemade muffins, cookies, cakes and puddings. They think big here: a "small" cafe au lait is big enough to fill a thermos. Sunday nights there is live music, which draws a local lesbian crowd.

St. Germaine Bakery-Cafe (1210 N. State Pkwy., 312/266-9900). Presentation is everything, and this bakery exhibits all the tortes, strudels and flans in such a way that you will want to try one of everything. Trust me.

Swedish Bakery (5348 N. Clark, 773/561-8919). A truly Scandinavian establishment with out-of-this-world marzipan, iced almond tarts and Swedish cookies. There are no tables, so don't plan to kick back and read a paper while you munch on your goodies. A 30-minute wait is common, even at 6:30 a.m.

🎵 PLAY-MEET

Annex 3 (3160 N. Clark, 773/327-5969). A predominantly gay and lesbian dance hall that doubles as a friendly place to watch a Sunday afternoon football game.

Berlin (954 W. Belmont, 773/348-4975). Multicultural, pansexual video dance club, open until 4 a.m. Women's Obsession happens on Wednesday nights.

Big Chicks (5024 N. Sheridan, 773/728-5511). A gay and lesbian dance club featuring daily food specials: jumbo hot dogs on Saturdays, and a Sunday afternoon buffet.

Club Intimus (312 W. Randolph, 773/901-1703). Mainly a bar for Afro-American women, and only on Saturday nights.

Girl Bar (2625 N. Halsted, 773/871-4210). A festive women's place to spend a Saturday night. Not a lot of seating, and the bar gets backed up easily, but the place definitely has more pizzazz than a neighborhood pub. Try the 16-ounce "Glowing Citron" cocktail.

Madrigal's (5316 N. Clark, 773/334-3033). An Andersonville neighborhood bar known for friendliness and great cheeseburgers.

Paris Dance (1122 W. Montrose, 773/769-0602). Though not as quaint as neighborhood bars, this old establishment is billed as Chicago's premier women's night club. Sister 2 Sister hosts "Paris Noir" for women of color on Thursdays.

Winners (4530 N. Lincoln Ave., 773/271-4378). Chicago's newest women's bar. Lesbian-owned and operated.

💲 SHOP

General Shopping

The heart of spectacular shopping is, of course, Chicago's Magnificent Mile, which runs along Michigan Avenue from Oak Street to the Chicago River. There you will find the big New York department stores such as Saks Fifth Avenue, Lord & Taylor and Bloomingdale's. But it is quickly becoming the Mediocre Three-Quarter Mile, what with the two

CHICAGO

fairly new, impressive, yet controversial vertical shopping malls that contain more than 200 shops and restaurants, and nine cinemas: **Chicago Place** (700 N. Michigan) and **600 N. Michigan Ave**. Oak Street, around the corner from Michigan Avenue, is where designs from Paris, Milan and Manhattan are mixed with Chicago's Gold Coast atmosphere. The result is an international street lined with intimate buildings and shops.

Food Markets

Though lacking a year-round central farmers' market, and deprived of fresh local produce for half the year, Chicago is still an ideal city for honing hunting-and-gathering skills. A plethora of ethnic food shops and grocery stores are scattered throughout the city's neighborhoods and suburbs. Here are a few to get your mouth watering:

North Pier Festival Market (435 E. Illinois St., 312/836-4300). A renovated building, formerly a shipping terminal, with three floors of unusual shops and restaurants.

Conte Di Savoia (1438 W. Taylor St., 312/666-3471). An original Italian grocery featuring different cold cuts, such as coppocollo, soppressa veneta, mortadello and, of course, prosciutto.

Whole Foods Market (1000 W. North Ave., 773/587-0648). There are five additional locations of this gigantic natural foods supermarket scattered throughout Chicagoland. This one is located in the heart of Lakeview.

Secondhand Stores

George's Antiques and Vintage (5308 N. Clark, 773/784-7080). There's no store sign out front, but you can easily identify the shop by the nicely placed junk in the window. No price is set in stone. George will barter with you, and, if asked politely, he will show you his exquisite, downstairs vintage clothing collection.

Pride Shopping

Gay Mart (3457 N. Halsted, 773/929-4272). If it's queer, it's here.

The Paper Trail (5307 N. Clark, 773/275-2191). A card and party supply store that also has an assortment of rainbow paraphernalia.
We're Everywhere (3434 N. Halsted, 773/404-0590). Gay-designed T-shirts, sweats, shorts, hats and accessories.

Clothing

Jalan-Jalan Boutique (5317 N. Clark, 773/989-5674). An unexpected extension of Kopi's Cafe, featuring art, jewelry, clothing and travel gear from around the world.
Studio 90 (5239 N. Clark, 773/878-0097). Artistic woman-made clothing, jewelry and accessories next door to the Woman Wild gallery.

Galleries

Woman Made Gallery (4646 N. Rockwell, 773/588-4317). This treasure trove features women's art exhibits, as well as a permanent display of paintings and other artifacts.
Woman Wild Treasures by Women (5237 N. Clark, 773/878-0300). A unique store with handmade items from more than 125 women artists. Heavily lesbian.

Bookstores

Afrocentric Bookstore (234 S. Wabash, 312/939-1956). A unique center for Chicago's African-American community. The inventory stretches from books to T-shirts, cards, African-American jewelry, posters and figurines.
Prairie Moon (8 N. Dunton Ave., Arlington Heights, 708/342-9608). The northwest suburbs' well-endowed feminist bookstore. Cards, T-shirts, jewelry and cassettes. The walls are lined with local women's paintings and sculptures. Definitely worth the trip, especially on your way to or from O'Hare airport.
Pride Agenda (1109 Westgate, Oak Park, 708/524-UGAY). Gay and lesbian bookstore in the beautiful suburb of Oak Park.

CHICAGO

Unabridged Books (3251 N. Broadway, 773/833-9119). A carefully selected line of general interest books. Featured titles include gay and lesbian interest, literature, cooking and children's books.

Women and Children First (5233 N. Clark, 773/769-9299). One of America's most comprehensive feminist bookstores, featuring frequent author events and a community bulletin board. There is a basket of toys to occupy the little ones while you browse.

🦋 KIDS' STUFF

Brookfield Zoo (First Ave. and 31st St., Brookfield, 708/485-0263). Features naturalistic and multispecies exhibits in a mostly cageless environment: Tropic World is a full-scale re-creation of tropical rainforests around the world, and the Swamp is modeled after a southern cypress swamp and an Illinois wetland.

Lincoln Park Zoo (2200 N. Cannon, 312/742-2000). One of the only remaining free city zoos, the urban site on the North Side near the lake devotes 35 acres to more that 2200 exotic critters.

Museum of Science and Industry (57th St. at Lake Shore Dr., 312/684-1414). Thousands of exhibits demonstrate scientific principles, technical advances and industrial applications.

Shedd Aquarium (1200 S. Lake Shore Dr., 312/939-2438). The world's largest indoor aquarium with beluga whales, Pacific white-sided dolphins and Alaskan sea otters.

☼ SPIRITUAL

Archidiocesan Gay and Lesbian Outreach (690 Belmont, 312/525-3872). Catholic Mass every Sunday at 7 p.m.

Congregation Or Chadash (656 W. Barry, 312/248-9456). Jewish gay men and lesbians; all are welcome.

Dignity Chicago (3344 N. Broadway, 773/296-0780). Catholic gay men and lesbians Mass every Sunday at 7 p.m., followed by a social hour.

Holy Trinity Lutheran Church (1218 W. Addison, 773/248-1233).

Integrity Chicago (312/348-6362). Gay and lesbian Episcopalian group.

MCC of the Resurrection (5540 S. Woodlawn, 312/288-1535).

PLGC (600 W. Fullerton, 312/784-2635). Presbyterian gay men and lesbians.

Unitarian Universalist Lesbian and Gay Concerns (656 W. Barry, 312/549-0260).

RESOURCES

General Information

Chicago Visitor's Bureau (800/226-6632).

Chicago Area Gay and Lesbian Chamber of Commerce (888/452-4262, www.glchamber.com).

Gerber-Hart Gay and Lesbian Library Archives (3352 N. Paulina, 773/883-3003). Offers a collection of gay and lesbian books, newspapers, historical documents and educational programming.

Kindred Hearts Women's Center (2214 Ridge, Evanston, 847/604-0931).

Lesbian and Gay Help Line (773/929-HELP).

Out Chicago (www.outchicago.org). A thorough Internet resource for gays and lesbians.

Women of the Western Suburbs (708/622-4327). WOWS — a social group of 300 lesbians — meets the fourth Sunday of every month.

Women's AIDS Project (5249 N. Kenmore, 773/271-2242).

Women's Place Resource Center (312/553-9008).

Women's Program of Howard Brown Health Center (945 W. George, 773/871-5777 ext. 200). Primary care health services for lesbian and bisexual women.

CHICAGO

Media

Black Lines (773/871-7610). Monthly magazine for the lesbian, gay and bisexual African American community.

Diversity Radio. Sundays, 10 a.m. to noon, on WCBR-FM 92.7.

New City (312/243-8786, www.newcitynet.com). Chicago's newest weekly entertainment newspaper.

Nightlines (773/871-7610). A weekly publication for the gay and lesbian community that focuses on the night life.

Outlines (773/871-7610, www.suba.com/~outlines). A monthly community newsletter look-at-a-glance.

Windy City Times (312/397-0025). The main Chicago gay and lesbian weekly.

Los Angeles, California

area codes 213 & 310

WHAT TO EXPECT

Remember how your feet used to feel after hours and hours of roller skating? You would rest for a while, and it *still* felt like you were buzzing along on the concrete, feeling the bumps, cracks and spinning wheels under your feet. It's like that in Los Angeles, too, except folks have graduated from roller skates to automobiles. And after hours on the freeway, you feel as though you are *still* moving at warp speed. It makes it hard to be stationary. As a tourist in L.A., there's that "I can't sit still because I might miss something" feeling all the time.

Los Angeles is a great place to vacation with children. Chances are that everything that appeals to you, as an adult, will have some kind of appeal to the younger set, as well. Hey, it's the home of the entertainment industry. What do you expect? Hollywood's rich and famous, fantastic sports cars and movie industry has lured tourists worldwide. As the entertainment mogul, L.A. has never let us down. Even the billboards along Sunset Boulevard are worth a second look.

West Hollywood, south of Sunset Boulevard, is one of the *trés* gayest cities in the world, and is inhabited mostly by men. Yet, as the rainbow flags appear along Santa Monica Boulevard's median, it's hard for a lesbian to *not* feel some sort of connection to the place. It's worth parking the car and wandering in and out of the gay-owned stores. Eventually, you'll come upon Little Frida's coffee house — probably the most visible lesbian hangout in West Hollywood. Little Frida's is not just a java stop, though. Most evenings there is some sort of live entertainment: women musicians, comediennes or poetry readings.

During the day, Little Frida's sometimes hosts a "pet fest," at which time the small place is infested with dykes and their dogs. And every now and then, Little Frida's will co-sponsor a shindig at West Hollywood's all-important Gay and Lesbian Center.

The lesbian communities are, of course, off the tourist's beaten path. Many women claim there is not a "lesbian neighborhood" at all, but that lesbians are just all over the place. That's probably true in this area of some 30 cities — not suburbs — packed together like sardines, with each city having its own women's community. Spots in which lesbians make up a bigger part of the population are Silver Lake, Pasadena, Long Beach — also known as "Lavender Beach" — and Laguna Beach. There are also substantial lesbian communities in Westwood, Santa Monica and Venice, though not as visible.

Basically, on any given day, there are two different ways of keying into the Los Angeles lesbian scene: either go to the beaches, or go to the bars. Dance clubs are popular in L.A., and since they don't compete with each other on most nights, there's usually only one place to go that's also attracting the rest of the city's women. The beaches are also popular with women. "Mother's Beach," located on Long Beach, in Alamitos Bay just north of Second and Naples Island, is perfect for young children because of the lack of waves and pebbles. And, if being sedentary at the beach is not your cup of tea, don't worry because there are miles and miles of shoreline paths for in-line skating, walking, jogging or bicycling. In Los Angeles, it's not difficult to get that cement back under your feet.

What To Bring

Trendy and retro work well: 1950's-style pointed sunglasses and Hawaiian shirts, or skimpy spaghetti-strapped dresses with platform shoes. Accessorize with a water bottle and holster slung over your shoulder.

Best Time To Visit

April skies are the clearest after winter rains, and bougainvillea is in full bloom.

LOS ANGELES

Getting There

Every major airline flies to Los Angeles International Airport. And there are several other airports in the vicinity, including the John Wayne Airport in Orange County, as well as airports in Burbank, Ontario and Long Beach— although LAX offers the best prices.

Getting Around

Rent a car. After all, you are what you drive. **Beverly Hills Rent-A-Car** (800/479-5996) rents Jaguars, Corvettes, Rolls Royces, Bentley's and Vipers by the hour, with complimentary cellular phones.

STAY

Guest Houses

Country Comfort B&B (5104 E. Valencia Dr., Anaheim, 714/532-4010). A lesbian-owned getaway seven miles east of Disneyland, and the only *known* lesbian-owned Bed & Breakfast in the entire megalopolis. A comfortable place. Three rooms, $65 each.

Hilltop House (3307 Bonnie Hill Dr., 883-0073). A gay-owned glass-walled guest suite in Hollywood Hills, with unblocked views of the canyons and valley. Secluded, comfortable and completely equipped for short- and long-term stays, and only a few minutes from the roar of the city. Sleeps up to four, with a private entrance and kitchen, as well as use of the pool and Jacuzzi. Very lesbian friendly. $120 per night; $500 per week.

SEE-DO

In and Around Los Angeles

El Pueblo de Los Angeles Historic Park (800 N. Alameda, 638-6987). This is the place where Los Angeles was founded. Many of the original buildings can be found on **Olvera Street**, the heart of the city, accompanied by Mexican-American music, food and shopping.

Getty Center (405 Freeway and Sunset Blvd., 310/440-7300). Looking like a 21st century castle at the top of a hill, this grand museum can be seem from miles away. The museum houses a permanent collection of Greek and Roman antiquities, drawings, sculptures, and 19th and 20th century European and American photographs.

Hollywood. There is enough to do in Hollywood to fill an entire vacation. However, you might want to minimize activities there, in order to maximize your time at the beach. **Hollywood Fantasy Tours** (469-8184 or 800/782-7287) or **Casablanca Sightseeing** (461-0156) is a great way to view the stars's homes in Hollywood Hills and the city of Los Angeles. Check out the **Frederick's of Hollywood Lingerie Museum** (6608 Hollywood Blvd., 466-8506) displaying vintage movie star accoutrements dating from 1946, and housing a gigantic lingerie shop. And make sure to see a first-run film at the state-of-the-art **Hollywood Galaxy Theaters** (7021 Hollywood Blvd., 957-9246).

June L. Mazer Lesbian Archives (626 N. Robertson Blvd., West Hollywood, 659-2478). An inexhaustible collection of lesbian-only writings, posters, videos and audio tapes, with featured readings and lectures. Call ahead for an appointment.

Los Angeles Conservancy Walking Tours (623-CITY). Time to get out of the car. The conservancy, which plays an important role in preserving the city's architectural heritage and historic landmarks, conducts 11 different walking tours on Saturdays. A few include "Little Tokyo," "Art Deco," "Pershing Square" and "Broadway Theaters." $5.

Museum of Neon Art (501 W. Olympic Blvd., 489-9918). The museum houses permanent exhibits, and conducts monthly bus tours of the area's historic neon signs and movie marquees.

Natural History Museum of Los Angeles County (900 Exposition, 744-3466). Houses 15 million specimens, most of which were gathered from the Los Angeles tar pits.

Off 'N Running Tours (310/246-1418). With a vigorous, five-mile jog, this tour takes in several cityscapes, most of which are in the Beverly Hills area.

LOS ANGELES

Near Los Angeles

Beach Cities. Go west, young woman! Santa Monica Beach is a great place to start. Rent in-line skates or bicycles and roll south on the 22-mile boardwalk that ends in Ranchos Palos Verdes. Venice Beach offers a more dog-oriented crowd. In fact, dog owners have been fighting for their own Dog Beach. Do your next workout at one of Muscle Beach's outdoor gyms. Or stop at Manhattan Beach for a quick volleyball game. Morning visits to any beach are best for avoiding off-shore winds and crowds.

Catalina Island can be reached either by **Catalina Passenger Service** (673-5245) or on a tour with **Catalina Cruises** (800/228-2546). It's 26 miles across the sea to swimming, snorkeling, scuba diving, kayaking and hiking trails.

Griffith Park (Ranger headquarters, 4730 Crystal Springs, 665-5188). Located in the Santa Monica Mountains, it one of the largest urban parks in the country, and an all-day affair. Visit the **Autry Museum of Western Heritage** (at the junction of Golden State and Ventura freeways, 667-2000), which pays homage to the American West. Or follow various hiking trails to the **Griffith Observatory** (664-1191), the famous "Hollywood" letters, wagon rides and a miniature train.

Hiking. It's the latest rage. Try Fryman Canyon in Hollywood Hills, near the corner of Fryman Road and Laurel Canyon Boulevard in Studio City. Solstice Canyon near Malibu is filled with wildflowers and water falls. Charmlee Nature Preserve near Topanga Canyon is covered with wildflowers in the spring. And several trails in the Topanga Canyon area offer views of the city, as well as a sense of serenity. Call **Mountain Parks Information Service** (800/533-7275).

KEEP FIT-RECREATION

Los Angeles Frontrunners (460-2554). Every Thursday meet at the fountain at Doheny and Santa Monica Blvd. for a fun run, 6:30 p.m.

Women on a Roll (310/578-8888). It's not just a bicycling club. The group also meets for Bingo, river rafting, in-line skating, dog walks and wine tasting. Women of all fitness levels and muscle mass are welcome. Call for a newsletter.

Women Who Run With Women (993-7443). Runners and walkers of all levels meet every Sunday, 9 a.m., in front of the Recreation Center at 14201 Huston.

EAT

Fine Dining

Michael's (1147 Third St., Santa Monica, 310/451-0843). The Southern California cuisine revolution of the 1980s took a turn for the better when Michael's entered the scene. The patio is one of the city's most beautiful settings for a meal. $15-50.

Spago (8795 Sunset Blvd., 310/652-4025). Known for its inventive pizzas, Wolfgang Puck's first restaurant also serves foie gras, risotto, crab spring rolls and roast venison. Reservations are required for the celebrity-infested dining room. $10-40.

Casual Dining

Antonio's (7470 Melrose Ave., 655-0480). Antonio's was serving authentic south-of-the-border cuisine before Melrose became an Avenue. The traditional Oaxacan Camarones Enchiladas are excellent. Lesbian friendly.

Big Cup (7965 Beverly at Fairfax, 653-5358). The breakfast linguine is a delicious mound of chicken-and-egg-coated noodles; the seven-grain and granola pancakes are the epitome of health; and, yes, coffee is served in a huge container.

Carney's (8351 Sunset Blvd., 654-8300). One of the cheapest, but tastiest meals on the famous Strip. Don't miss the soft chicken tacos on corn tortillas, or the chocolate-dipped, frozen banana dessert. Lesbian friendly. $1-4.

Thai Dishes (10926 W. Pico Blvd., 310/470-4559). The tasty flavor of Thailand is indisputably captured on these cheaper plates. And the Pad Thai reigns supreme. $6-15.

LOS ANGELES

Van Go's Ear (796 Main St., Venice Beach, 310/314-0022). Owned by "lesbian chicks with British accents," who cater to the casual Venice Beach crowd. Open 24 hours. Weekend brunches draw a large lesbian crowd. $3-7.

Westwood Brewing Company (1097 Glendon Ave., 310/209-2739). Typical brew-pub burger and salad fare. It's best to be there on a sunny late summer afternoon to watch the sun set, while drinking a cold brewski. $5-12.

Coffeehouses

Little Frida's (8730 Santa Monica Blvd., 310/854-5421, www.casenet.com/coffeehouse/fridascalendar). This is *the* West Hollywood lesbian hot spot. The coffee shop-bakery is expanding its menu to include sandwiches and hot dishes, while keeping tow on the women's scene as a gallery, a place for writers, musicians and comediennes.

♫ PLAY-MEET

Bars

Club 3772 (3772 E. Foothill Blvd., Pasadena, 818/578-9359). A casual, friendly lesbian bar in the Valley. Live music is the second major attraction.

Connection (4363 Sepulveda Blvd., West Los Angeles, 310/391-6817). A neighborhood lesbian club on the west side, with a pool table, DJ and dancing. Friendly clientele.

Rumors (10622 Magnolia, North Hollywood, 818/506-9651). Friendly, down-to-earth neighborhood women's bar on the north side.

The Huntress (8122 Bolsa, Midway City, 714/892-0048). Orange County's lesbian bar, open seven days a week.

The Palms (8572 Santa Monica Blvd., West Hollywood, 310/652-6188). L.A.'s most popular women's bar. Sexual tension is hot, and babe-watching is primo. The last Monday of every month features women's short films and videos.

Night Clubs

Fuel (hotline, 310/626-5659). A Sunday women's night club presented by 2 City Girlz with D.J. Kickin' K.

Girl Bar (hotline, 460-2531). Like a wandering minstrel show, Girl Bar shows up at different places around town for the hottest of lesbian night clubs.

Michelle's XXX (7969 Santa Monica Blvd., 654-0820). Women's dance and strip club on Tuesday nights. Fashionable dress code is enforced. Things start to happen around midnight.

Sappho Rainbow (20923 Roscoe Blvd., 818/341-8503). A Sunday night women's dance club at the huge Mancinis. Two full bars, pool and darts, DJ and a giant dance floor.

SHOP

General Shopping

Some of the best shopping in the world is in Los Angeles. **Rodeo Drive** (in Beverly Hills, between Wilshire and Santa Monica Blvd.) is the hottest spot. Okay, so you can't afford to buy that New Year's Eve Gucci gown or the Cartier suit, but it's still fun to look — and even more fun to try them on. **Beverly Boulevard** and **La Brea Avenue** (on and around Sixth St.) offer clusters of urban and eclectic antique furniture and vintage clothing stores, alternating with sidewalk cafes and trendy coffee shops. To shop for wilder things, try artsy **Melrose Avenue**, where you will find everything from thigh-high leather boots to vinyl, day-glow apparel and edible lingerie. Other hot spots are **Sunset Boulevard**, and **Main Street** and **Montana Avenue** in Santa Monica.

Food Markets

Farmers' Market (6333 W. Third St., 933-9211). With more than 120 shops, grocers, and the coveted free parking, this is a great place to nosh while shopping for L.A. souvenirs.

LOS ANGELES

Wild Oats (8611 Santa Monica Blvd., West Hollywood, 310/854-6927). The whole foods chain is situated in the heart of gay L.A.

Secondhand Stores

Recycled Rags (2731 E. Coast Hwy., Corona del Mar, 714/675-5553). The Rolls Royce of resale shops with glittering gowns, tuxedos, sportswear and sweaters.

Bookstores

A Different Light (8853 Santa Monica Blvd., 310/854-6601, www.adlbooks.com). The closest thing to a mainstream gay and lesbian bookstore, it's packed full of queer titles, as well as being well stocked with pride paraphernalia.

Alexandria II Bookstore (567 S. Lake Ave., 818/792-7885). The largest New Age bookstore in the San Gabriel Valley. Great selection of gems, crystals and reading materials.

Book Soup (8818 Sunset Blvd., 310/659-3110). L.A.'s literary set heads here for readings from locals such as Madonna. And the adjacent **Book Soup Bistro** (310/657-1072) appropriately dishes up hearty bowls of alphabet soup.

Page One (1200 E. Walnut, Pasadena, 818/796-8418). Complete women's bookstore serving the Valley community, and featuring readings and book discussion groups.

Sisterhood (1351 Westwood Blvd., 310/477-7300). Located in the collegiate neighborhood near UCLA, this women's bookstore can help you find anything, from fiction to chocolate. Check out the resource room.

🦋 KIDS' STUFF

Disneyland (1313 S. Harbor Blvd., Anaheim, 714/999-4565). Plan to spend at least a day at one of the more classic, and classy amusement parks. A one-day Magic ticket costs $34.

Los Angeles Children's Museum (310 N. Main St., 687-8800). Kids can produce their own television news show.

Pacific Park (Santa Monica Pier, Santa Monica, 310/260-8744). An amusement park situated entirely on the end of the pier with rides and games, including the original 1908 hand-carved carousel.

Universal Studios (100 Universal City Plaza, 818/508-9600). A wild, Hollywood-esque theme park.

SPIRITUAL

Beth Chayim Chadashim (10345 W. Pico Blvd., 931-7023). A synagogue serving the lesbian community.

Calvary Open Door (514 W. Katella, Orange, 714/284-5775).

Dignity Los Angeles (126 S. Ave. 64, 344-8064). Catholic mass 5:30 p.m. Sundays.

MCC of the Valley (5730 Cahuenga Blvd., 818/762-1133). 10 a.m. Sunday service.

MCCLA (8714 Santa Monica Blvd., 310/854-9110). Early Sunday service, 9 a.m.; also service at 11 a.m.; evening service, 6 p.m.; and Spanish-language service, 12:30 p.m.

RESOURCES

General information

Los Angeles Visitor Information (685 S. Figueroa St., 689-8822).

West Hollywood Convention & Visitors Bureau (8687 Melrose Ave., Suite M-26, 310/289-2525 or 800/368-6020).

Audre Lorde Lesbian Health Clinic (1625 N. Schrader Blvd., 993-7570). Housed in the Gay and Lesbian Center.

Cultural Affairs Department (688-ARTS). A 24-hour hotline with the latest information about festivals, art shows, theater and music events.

Gay and Lesbian Community Center (1625 Schrader Blvd., 993-7400).

LOS ANGELES

LAAPIS (696-4084). Los Angeles Asian Pacific Islander Sisters meet for potlucks, social outings and workshops. Call for a monthly newsletter.

Lesbian Dining Club (310/364-4616). A monthly dining, and sometimes dancing, singles social outing.

Media

fab! (655-5716). A lesbian and gay biweekly magazine of local activities.

Girl Guide (310/391-8877). Thorough coverage of monthly lesbian events and issues.

Party Talk. Gay and lesbian video magazine show, Sundays, channel 28, 11 p.m.

LA Weekly (465-9909, www.laweekly.com). An exhaustive list of local happenings and movie reviews, and mostly straight news and features.

Blade (714/376-9880, http://ocblade.com). The Orange County and Long Beach gay and lesbian monthly news magazine.

Lesbian News (310/787-8658, or 800/458-9888). The premier lesbian monthly, which is heavy on "lesbian" and slight on "news."

Festivals and Events

Outfest (782-1125, www.outfest.com). The 10-day Los Angeles gay and lesbian film festival of documentaries, shorts, features, panels and special events, which usually takes place the second week of July at the Director's Guild of America, in Hollywood.

LONG BEACH (AREA CODE 310)

Twenty-two miles south of Los Angeles lies the popular lesbian neighborhood of Long Beach, also known as "Lavender Beach."

Metro Blue Line (213/626-4455). Starts at the downtown Seventh

Street-Metro Station and continues south through Huntington Park, Compton, and ends at Long Beach. The light rail runs every six to 15 minutes, depending on the time of day, and travel time is 45 minutes.

SEE-DO

In and Around Long Beach

Queen Mary (1126 Queens Highway, 435-3511). It sounds like a place gay men would frequent, but it's actually a great ocean liner to hang out on and learn a bit of history, shop, dine, and, of course, bungee jump. That's right, **Mega Bungee** (435-1880) is the tallest bungee tower in North America. At 21 stories high, it hangs over San Pedro Bay.

PLAY-MEET

Bars

Que Sera (1923 E. Seventh St., 599-6170). Long Beach's most popular women's night club. Open seven nights a week, but things don't really rock until the weekends.

SHOP

Pine Avenue between Ocean and Seventh is getting hotter and hipper all the time, with trendy shops and bistros. **Pearl's Booksellers** (224 Redondo Blvd., 438-8875) is the area's only women-owned, lesbian-feminist bookstore. Nearby **By the Book** (2501 E. Broadway, 930-0088) is an alternative bookstore specializing in lesbian and women's studies.

RESOURCES

Gay and Lesbian Community Services Center (2017 E. Fourth

LOS ANGELES

St., 434-4455).
Long Beach Visitors Bureau (1 World Trade Center, Suite 300, 436-3645).

LAGUNA BEACH (Area Code 714)

Located between Orange County and San Diego, Laguna Beach is becoming a hot gay and lesbian vacation destination, not to mention the growing community that the area houses year-round.

STAY

Cottage (368 Oak St., 497-3695). This two-bedroom, gay-owned bungalow is for rent only by the week. It is a private house one block from the beach and two blocks from the lesbian-owned Viktor/Viktoria Italian restaurant and bar. $700 per week.
Casa Laguna Inn (2510 S. Coast Hwy., 494-2996 or 800/233-0449). A Spanish-style B&B overlooking the Pacific Ocean. Complimentary afternoon wine and hors d'oeuvres. Lesbian friendly. $95-130.

SEE-DO

In and Around Laguna Beach

Festival of the Arts and Pageant of the Masters (494-1145). A mid-summer celebration of the arts in Laguna Beach.
Festival of the Whales (in Dana Point, 496-1555). Between mid-February and early-March, California gray whales migrate from the Arctic to their breeding grounds in Mexico. Commercial cruises are available for tours, but it's also possible to view the leviathans with binoculars from ocean bluffs.
Laguna Art Museum (307 Cliff Dr., 494-8971). A collection of American art with a focus on California. The museum store sells a wide

variety of items, including books, toys and jewelry.

Laguna Playhouse (606 Laguna Canyon Rd., 494-8021). One of the region's premier professional theater companies.

EAT

Viktor/Viktoria (1305 So. Pacific Coast Hwy., 376-8809). A delicious, lesbian-owned Italian restaurant. The manicotti is a good bet. $5-15.

Leap of Faith (1440 S. Coast Hwy., 494-8595). A very lesbian friendly bistro, elegantly serving everything from coffee and pastries, to sandwiches, dinner entrees and wine. Breakfast served on weekends. $2-10.

SHOP

Bookstore

A Different Drummer (1294-C S. Coast Hwy., 497-6699). A lesbian-owned women's bookstore located on a very visible corner.

RESOURCES

Laguna Beach Visitors Bureau (714/497-9229).

Minneapolis, Minnesota

area code 612

WHAT TO EXPECT

Minneapolis may not be first on anyone's list of "great vacation destinations," but that's only because of the horror stories that come from its cover-every-inch-of-your-face-or-it-may-freeze-and-fall-off winters. I lived in the city of lakes for three years, and it *did* take me that long to acquire a mere part of the winter wardrobe that I needed in order to subsist comfortably, including a full face mask and silk long undies — all of which support the saying that there are only two seasons in Minneapolis: winter and winter preparation.

In retrospect, I admit that the six- to seven-month-long winter really is the season in which the city blossoms. All of the preparation that goes into building indoor amusement parks, gargantuan shopping malls, heated sidewalks, miles and miles of skyways, and automobile battery plug-ins in public parking lots — all the things that seem useless, over-built and excessive during the hot and humid, mosquito-infested summer months — actually pays off. Each winter the place goes through a metamorphosis during which its many lush parks become iced-over skating and hockey rinks, bicycle paths become cross-country ski routes, and lakes become home to thousands of ice fishing communities.

The state motto rings true: "Cold feet, but a warm heart." Minnesotans love the sub-zero temperatures and seem to thrive in the wind chill. It makes them feel alive and gives their lives challenge and purpose. I knew a woman who walked a half-mile to the ice cream shop whenever the temperature dropped to 20 below, never mind the wind chill. She would buy a double-dip cone, stick it in her pocket, walk home, and *then* eat it.

Warm hearts are the key ingredients of the city's thriving lesbian community. South Minneapolis' Powerderhorn Park — also known as Dyke Heights — houses more subscribers to the international newsletter "The Lesbian Connection" than any other zip code (55407). And the city is so politically liberal and progressive that the lesbian and straight communities have successfully integrated beyond the boundaries of Powderhorn Park and south Minneapolis, and into the entire city. Lesbians are everywhere! Possibly, Minneapolis lesbians invented the trademark coiffure of an almost-shaved head around the back, short above the ears, and mane-ish on the top. It's been the style there for at least 15 years.

A city rich in female energy, Minneapolis is surrounded by several memorials of historical, as well as fictitious women — never mind that most are associated with the city's surrounding waterways. For instance, Minnehaha Falls was named after the Native American wife of Hiawatha; Lake Nokomis was Hiawatha's grandmother; Lake Harriet was the wife of Colonel Leavenworth, who built Fort Snelling at the confluence of the Mississippi and Minnesota Rivers; and St. Anthony Falls to the north of downtown is supposedly haunted by the spirit of Native American Ampata Sapa. Grieving that her husband had left her to marry another woman, Ampata intentionally jumped over the falls with her children. Legend has it that her ghost still lingers in its mists.

Looking at a map, Powderhorn Park sits in the geographic center of it all. One can only imagine the legends that will emerge from there.

What To Bring

In the summer T-shirts, shorts and sunglasses are all you will need. During the winter months, bring long underwear, snow boots, a face mask, wool sweater, down mittens, wool hat, and a long wool or down coat. Make sure that you can cover every inch of skin. Obviously, fashion goes by the wayside this time of year.

Best Time To Visit

Minneapolis is in all of its winter glory in early February after the annual January thaw, but before the St. Paul Winter Carnival's ice sculptures melt completely.

MINNEAPOLIS

Getting Around

The city buses, **MTC** (349-7000), will take you any place you need to go, plus you won't have to worry about your car being too cold to start, or having to scrape windows. But in mild weather, renting a car is the best option.

STAY

Luxury

Nicollet Island Inn (95 Merriam St., 331-1800). A charming, country-style inn and restaurant on an island in the Mississippi River. Different packages are available for different degrees of romance, including champagne, fruit baskets, Jacuzzi suites and brunch for two. Lesbian friendly $115-280.

Guest Houses

Hotel Amsterdam (828 Hennepin Ave., 288-0459). Located downtown near the Gay 90s club. It's primarily gay boys that stay here, but lesbians are definitely welcome. $35-60.

Nan's Bed & Breakfast (2304 Fremont Ave. S., 377-5118 or 800/214-5118). Located in the Lake of the Isles and Guthrie Theatre neighborhood, the old house is a cozy nesting place. Lesbian friendly; children welcome. $40-50, includes a full breakfast.

SEE-DO

In and Around Minneapolis

Guthrie After 6 (725 Vineland Place, 377-2224). Minneapolis's premier show place, the Guthrie Theatre, offers a series of performances exclusively for the gay and lesbian community.

Mall of America (in Bloomington at Hwy. 494 and Cedar Ave., 851-3500). It's big enough to hold 32 Boeing 747s, and has a total storefront footage of 4.3 miles. A daily pickup of more than 6000 pounds of restaurant-food waste goes to feed 2000 pigs. All in all, it is a sensory overload that shouldn't be missed.

Minneapolis Institute of Arts (2400 Third Ave. S., 870-3131). Houses a collection of more than 85,000 objects from prehistoric to modern times.

Old Arizona Studio (2821 Nicollet Ave., 871-0050). This place is great! Live music, dance and theater productions. You'll want to arrive early for something to eat from the cafe and mingle with the crowd. Lesbian-owned.

Theatre de la Jeune Lune (105 N. First St., 333-6200). Quirky, yet professional, this theater troupe offers some of the zaniest performances in contemporary theater.

The Lakes (south of Hwy. 212, north of Hwy. 494, west of Hwy. 35W and east of Hwy. 101). Surrounding the city are six lakes — Brownie, Cedar, Lake of the Isles, Calhoun, Harriet and Nokomis — that form an "urban wilderness" area. All are connected by bike paths, or you can canoe from one lake to the next. The canoe waters end at Minnehaha Falls near Lake Nokomis. There is a bird refuge near Lake Harriet, as well as a rose garden. In the winter, bring ice skates to Lake of the Isles, or rent them in the warming hut along Lake of the Isles Parkway.

Vulva Riot (349-1868). A monthly all-women multi-media cabaret. Anything goes, from mellow guitar duets to comedy acts. Show times are unpredictable, though. Call ahead for schedule. $5-sliding scale.

Walker Art Center and Minneapolis Sculpture Garden (725 Vineland Pl., 375-7600). Permanent collection of modern art adjacent to the largest urban sculpture garden in the U.S. The Walker offers "Dyke Night" during Gay Pride Week.

Women's History Bus Tour (739-7953). Sponsored by the Franciscan Holistic Center, the tour offers everything you might want to know about women's history in the Twin Cities. Tour times vary, so call ahead. The six-hour, $35 ride includes guide, bus and lunch.

Near Minneapolis

Boundary Waters Canoe Area. In a pristine wilderness area

MINNEAPOLIS

along the Minnesota-Canada border, it is a canoeist's dreamland. In winter, it transforms into a cross-country skiing winter wonderland. While there, stay at **Rainbow Island** (473-7889), a lesbian-owned retreat on a 10-acre island. It rents by the week and comes with the use of a canoe. Nightly, $130-150; weekly, $850-950.

Minnesota History Center (345 Kellogg Blvd. W., St. Paul, 296-6126). A good look at the state's history up close and personal: includes vintage Betty Crocker radio broadcasts — because you've been wondering what her voice *really* sounds like.

Prairie Home Companion (at the Fitzgerald Theater in St. Paul, 10 Exchange St., 290-1221). If Garrison Keillor is in town, don't miss his impressive radio show. Tickets are $16-25, and are on sale at the theater's box office or at Ticket Master (989-5151).

Ramsey County Courthouse and St. Paul City Hall (Wabasha and Fourth St., 266-8694). An impressive 1930s Art Deco structure, this originally $4 million building recently received a $49 million face lift. Free, self-guided tours are available.

Science Museum of Minnesota (30 E. 10th St., St. Paul, 221-2517). Creative, hands-on natural science exhibits. Check out the Omni Theater.

KEEP FIT-RECREATION

Frontrunners and Walkers (724-2211). Meets Sundays at 10 a.m., or Thursday evenings at 6:30 p.m. at Lake Calhoun.

Woodswomen (800/279-0555). The national women's outdoor tour company puts together many outings near the Minneapolis area.

Women in the Wilderness (227-2284). And this tour group does, too. Several of these trips are geared for women and children.

EAT

Fine Dining

Campiello (1320 W. Lake St., 825-2222). Wood-oven-cooked pizzas, short ribs and sea bass make this a popular and exquisite Uptown

69

eatery. $8-20.

New French Cafe (124 N. Fourth St., 338-3790). A Minneapolis tradition. The weekend brunch, yolk-only-with-cream omelets are not for the cholesterol conscious. Add asparagus and gruyere to top it off. Dinners are even better. Woman-owned; very lesbian friendly. $6-20.

Casual Dining

Cafe Wyrd (1600 W. Lake St., 827-5710). There are no sandwiches at this lunch stop, only a soup and salad of the day. Stark decor, and well-heated in the winter. Coffee drinks, as well. Lesbian-owned. $2-5.

It's Greek To Me (626 W. Lake St., 825-9922). Buttery spanakopita, hummus, dolmas and fresh tabouli salad served in a bright restaurant at the corner of Lake and Lyndale. Popular with lesbians. $3-14.

La Covina (1570 Selby Ave., St. Paul, 645-5288). Used to be that you couldn't get *any* Mexican food in Minnesota, but now the lesbian community has come to the rescue and opened this cozy cantina. Lesbian-owned. $6-10.

May Day Cafe (3440 Bloomington Ave. S., 729-5627). Mostly vegetarian fare: black bean and jasmine rice salad, burritos, hummus sandwiches, and baked goods are fresh from their oven. Located near Powderhorn Park. Lesbian-owned. $3-7.

Old Arizona Cafe (2821 Nicollet Ave., 871-0050). This lesbian-owned cafe offers light fare, beer and wine for pre-theater goers. There are always several women on the premises. $3-8.

Ruby's Cafe (1614 Harmon Place, 338-2089). Located next door to the Amazon Bookstore, and open early for breakfast. Also stays open late for the after-hours bar crowd. Every egg entree is named after a famous woman. Lesbian-owned. $3-9.

Coffeehouses

Blue Moon Coffee Cafe (3822 E. Lake St., 721-9230). The last chance to fill up with java before crossing the river into St. Paul.

MINNEAPOLIS

Features live music and readings. $1-5.

Cahoots Coffee Bar (1562 Selby Ave., in St. Paul, 644-6778). Look for the rainbow flag in the window. Lesbian-owned. $1-5.

♪ PLAY-MEET

Club Metro (733 Pierce Butler, in St. Paul, 489-0002). A lesbian-owned acoustic bar with a concert area for live music. Draws a younger crowd. Weekend nights, it's "Dyke-o-rama."

Gay 90s (408 Hennepin Ave., 333-7755). A Minneapolis institution that has grown into a huge complex featuring three dance floors: the Annex, blasting techno-pop house music; the retro, 1970's upstairs lounge; and the main floor, featuring R&B. Mixed gay and lesbian.

Townhouse (1415 University Ave., St. Paul, 646-7087). Gay men and women, country-western.

💲 SHOP

General shopping

Calhoun Square (at the corner of Lake St. and Hennepin Ave., 824-1240). One-of-a-kind stores and cafes in the heart of the Uptown neighborhood.

Mall of America (see "See/Do"). If you need a mall fix, this should take care of it for the rest of your life.

Nicollet Mall (Nicollet Ave. between Washington Ave. and 12th St.). Downtown Minneapolis is peppered with Dayton's, Donaldson's and many other big department stores. There are also unique shops along Hennepin and First Avenues downtown, as well as in the Uptown area of Lake and Hennepin Streets. Shop 'till you drop, as there is no sales tax on clothing.

Food Markets

Minnesotans wholeheartedly believe in the age-old tradition of shopping at community cooperatives. It seems there is a food co-op on every other corner, with most of them being vegetarian-oriented. One of the bigger stores is **Wedge Natural Foods Coop** (2105 Lyndale Ave.) near the Franklin and Lyndale intersection.

Secondhand Stores

Gabriela's Vintage Clothing (1404 W. Lake St., 822-1512). Caters to the drag queen wardrobe. Boas, tiaras, that kind of thing.

Ragstock (1433 W. Lake St., 823-6690). Really cheap stuff, and piles of it.

Repeat Performance (707 W. 34th St.). There are many treasures at this lesbian-owned store.

Pride Shopping

Rainbow Road (109 W. Grant at LaSalle, Loring Park, 872-8448). Greeting cards, videos, and queer gifts for the queer at heart.

Bookstores

A Brother's Touch (2327 Hennepin Ave., 377-6279). A lesbian, gay and bisexual bookstore on the strip between downtown and Uptown.

Amazon Bookstore (1612 Harmon Place, 338-6560). A complete women's bookstore, including a used book section, jewelry, gifts, cards, posters and couches for hanging out.

Hungry Mind Bookstore (1648 Grand Ave., St. Paul, 699-0587). This impressive independent seller offers an extensive selection of titles in a casual setting.

The Book Shop of the Minnesota Women's Press (771 Raymond Ave., St. Paul, 646-3968). Feminist-oriented, yet there is something for everyone.

Winged One (2821 Nicollet Ave., 871-0050). A feminist- and spiritual-oriented bookstore and art space housed at the Old Arizona

MINNEAPOLIS

Studio. Lesbian-owned.

🦋 KIDS' STUFF

Camp Snoopy (at Mall of America, 883-8600). Minnesota's answer to Disney World. It is indoors and open year-round. After a few minutes of cotton candy and screaming carnival-goers, you will forget you are anywhere near a shopping center.

Children's Museum (10 W. Seventh St., 225-6000). A fairly new interactive center in downtown St. Paul.

Children's Theater (2400 Third Ave. S., 874-0400). The magical productions are the next best things to Broadway shows.

☼ SPIRITUAL

All God's Children MCC (3100 Park Ave., 824-2673).

Dignity Twin Cities (827-3103). Catholic gathering of gays and lesbians.

Integrity Twin Cities (317 17th Ave. SE, 825-2301).

St. Thomas Apostle Gay, Lesbian and Friends (2914 W. 44th St., 823-3823). Social Group meets last Sunday of every month.

Triangles Unitarian-Universalist (900 Mount Curve Ave., 374-9734). Meets the third Sunday of every month for a potluck.

☎ RESOURCES

General Information

Minneapolis Visitor's Bureau (33 S. Sixth St., 348-7000).

St. Paul Visitor's Bureau (55 E. Fifth St., 297-6985).

Bisexual Connection (3534 Girard Ave. N., 788-3702). Social and political group.

Chrysalis Women's Health Center (2650 Nicollett Ave., 871-0118).

Out to Brunch (391-3449). Women's social organization that dines out, goes bike riding and holds computer seminars.

Quatrefoil Library (1619 Dayton Ave., St. Paul, 641-0969). Lesbian, gay and bisexual lending library and resource center.

Women's Works (377-9114). Social club that sponsors a New Year's Eve dance, golf tournaments and other events.

Media

Dyke TV. Channel 32, 8:30 p.m. Mondays in Minneapolis, 10 p.m. Wednesdays in St. Paul.

Focus Point (288-9008). A weekly gay and lesbian newspaper with a heavy political beat, both locally and nationally.

Fresh Fruit. KFAI radio 90.3 FM, 7-8 p.m. Thursdays, 341-0980.

Green and Yellow TV. Cable Channel 6, 11 p.m. Thursdays.

Minnesota Women's Press (771 Raymond, St. Paul, 646-3968). A progressive monthly newspaper for all women, gay and straight.

Q Monthly (321-7300). A monthly paper that's heavy on features and entertainment listings for the male crowd.

Woodswomen News (800/279-0555). Newsletter and schedule distributed by the women's outdoor group.

Festivals

Aquatennial (331-8371). A water festival that takes place around the lakes area. After all, Minneapolis means "city of water."

Bastille Day. On July 14, the street party in the Warehouse District is the place for lesbians to see and be seen — especially with their dogs.

May Day. The annual spring festival takes place in Powderhorn Park, which is also known as "Dyke Heights."

Winter Carnival. The St. Paul celebration in January hales the dark months with a night parade, ice sculpture contests and general hoopla.

New Orleans, Louisiana

area code 504

WHAT TO EXPECT

Like the Mississippi River, creative juices have always flowed through New Orleans. Reading down the inexhaustible list of hometown boys is like reading a list of who's who in American arts: Tennessee Williams, Louis Armstrong, Paul Prudhomme, the Neville brothers, Wynton and Branford Marsalis, and Harry Connick Jr. — just to name a few. Every writer seems to have scribed a prize-winning story while overlooking a romantic alley from their rented flat in the French Quarter. Every gifted chef has either a TV cooking show, or a restaurant named after himself. And musicians still haunt the great jazz nightclubs, such as Snug Harbor and House of Blues. But after one glance through any guide book, the inevitable question is, "Aren't there any women in New Orleans?" Where are the Julia Childs and Koko Taylors? Admittedly, with male creativity oozing out of every 200-year-old crack in the floor boards, it can be difficult finding the women's community.

New Orleans is everybody's city, from the revelers who invade during Mardi Gras and Super Bowl, to the hordes of Fellini-esque nuns that frequent St. Louis Cathedral in Jackson Square. And many of the people who have helped make New Orleans "Festival Central" have either lived, worked or partied in the French Quarter, which has a Las Vegassy party-all-night-feel to it. And it has become, over the years, more of a neighborhood for gay men than lesbians.

But don't despair. The French Quarter's adjacent neighborhood Faubourg-Marigny (pronounced Merry-knee) is where the women are. Because this area lacks the tourist dollars of the Quarter, it is more repressed and run-down, but isn't short on charm. It is also a place to find free parking, since a coveted spot two blocks away will cost a whopping $8 an hour, money that can be better spent on *beignets* and café au laits at the Café du Monde in the historic French Market.

In this small, pie-shaped neighborhood there are three lesbian-owned guest houses, a gay and lesbian bookstore, and two lesbian-owned bars. A typical night out includes live jazz at Snug Harbor, then popping into the lesbian-owned Rubyfruit Jungle bar next door, where things begin rocking around midnight. The doors close at 3 a.m., but people continue partying until the bartender kicks everybody out at five or six o'clock in the morning. From there, it's a block-and-a-half walk to Peniche's twenty-four-hour restaurant for an early breakfast. A word of warning, though. Faubourg-Marigny doesn't have police on every corner after dark, as the French Quarter does. So, be leery of those dark, romantic alleys. You may find yourself being the subject of somebody's best-selling novel.

When you finally roll into bed at eight in the morning, don't think you are the only person in town doing so. New Orleans's neighborhoods are ghost towns until mid-afternoon. In fact, a typical Sunday brunch won't begin until 11 a.m. or 12 noon. — a testament to the city's motto: "Let the good times roll." And you might as well just go with the flow.

What To Bring

Anything goes, especially during Mardi Gras. Take a rain coat and a good pair of walking shoes. For a nice meal out, plan to dress up, as several upscale restaurants require it.

Best Time To Visit

Festival time is the best time to visit the Crescent City. The Mardi Gras "season" is from early January to the actual Mardi Gras day at the end of February. The popular Jazz & Heritage Festival is a 10-day celebration of Louisiana's unique culture that begins the end of April. Southern Decadence, which is a gay and lesbian blowout, happens over Labor Day weekend in September. The annual Great French Market Tomato Festival is in June, celebrating one of the South's most abundant vegetables. And, of course, the Super Bowl is in late January, that is, when New Orleans plays host.

Getting Around

There's no need for a rental car if you plan on staying in the French Quarter. To get there, take the **Airport Shuttle** (592-1991 or 800/543-6332), which serves the city's hotels and convention center. There is the free Canal Street ferry connecting the Quarter with the West Bank across the Mississippi. And all of the historic streetcars cost $1.25 a pop, and traverse the city along main tourist routes.

STAY

Luxury

Rosewalk House (320 Verret St., 368-1500). A fully catered B&B located across the river from the French Quarter via the free Canal Street ferry in the gay friendly neighborhood of Algiers. Claw-foot bath tub, fireplace with a cypress mantel, feather bed and full Creole breakfast. Go ahead, pamper yourself. $75.

The Cornstalk (915 Royal St., 523-1515). The mansion is named for its wrought-iron fence, which was hand-crafted into ears of corn to comfort a young 1800s bride who had moved from Iowa. A complimentary breakfast and newspaper can be enjoyed from the balcony. Lesbian friendly. $75-150.

Guest Houses

Bywater B&B (1026 Clouet St., 944-8438). Three rooms with king-sized beds in a remodeled double-shotgun house, and managed by an eccentric woman's nephew. Nice collection of Louisiana folk art to admire. It is about a mile walk through Faubourg-Marigny to the Quarter. Children and pets welcome. Lesbian-owned. $60-75.

Mentone B&B (1437 Pauger St., 943-3019). You will know it by its manicured facade. Five blocks from the French Quarter. Call about kids; no pets. Lesbian-owned. Two suites, $75-100.

Over "C's" (940 Elysian Fields, 943-7166). Suites in an old house furnished with king-sized beds, and located above Charlene's, a mellow women's bar. Within walking distance of the French Quarter. Lesbian-owned. $100.

SEE-DO

In and Around New Orleans

Anne Rice's Tours (592-0560). Yes, the author of "Interview with a Vampire" hailed from voodoo central. Where else could she have been so inspired? Three tours explore different facets of Rice's creative development, including a stroll through Lafayette Cemetery and a visit to Destrehan, the oldest Louisiana plantation, where scenes from "Interview" were filmed. $30-100.

Cookin' Cajun Cooking School (Store No. 116 in River Walk, 1 Poydras St., 586-8832). Two-hour demonstrations on preparing a full-course Cajun or Creole meal, such as andouille sausage jambalaya, fried eggplant fingers or shrimp remoulade. Your lunch will include whatever the chef cooks up. $17.50.

French Market-Flea Market (Esplanade and Decatur Streets, 596-3424). The Market sells everything for the Louisianan epicurean wannabe, as well as fresh shrimp, crawfish and produce. The attached flea market is the city's largest on-going garage sale. Buy your Mardi Gras beads here for the best deal.

French Quarter Walking Tour (523-3939). The quickest way to learn the ins and outs of the Quarter is to take this two-hour guided tour exploring its history, folklore and architecture. Price includes admission to two of four historic sites: the Louisiana State Museum, Presbytere, 1850 House, or the Old U.S. Mint. Adults, $10; children up to age 10, free.

Haunted History Walking Tour (723 St. Peter, 897-2030). The focus of these city tours are the legions of ghosts and vampires that are said to inhabit the French Quarter, and the ongoing voodoo scene that includes a visit to voodoo queen Marie Laveau's grave site. $15.

NEW ORLEANS

Louisiana Nature and Science Center (Joe W. Brown Memorial Park, 246-5672). An 86-acre wilderness park dedicated to the preservation of Louisiana's forests, wetlands and wildlife. Features hiking trails, wildlife exhibits, a wetland tour, and a laser and multimedia show. Adults, $4; children $2.

Mardi Gras World (233 Newton St., 361-7821). Take a look at the enormous floats being built for Carnival by touring this warehouse. Getting there is an adventure: Take the free Canal Street ferry to historic Algiers on the west side of the river where a shuttle will pick you up and take you the rest of the way. Adults, $5.50; children, $3.25.

Natchez Steamboat (586-8777 or 800/233-BOAT). On what Mark Twain called "wedding cakes on water," you can take a two-hour tour of the U.S.'s third largest port. Departs from the Toulouse Street Wharf across from Jackson Square. $15-21.

New Orleans Museum of Art (in City Park, 488-2631). In a city with a heavy French influence such as New Orleans you can count on the fine art museum having an impressive representation from the "Paris School," including Degas, Picasso, Dufy and Miró. $6.

Superdome Tours (587-3810). A look behind the scenes at the National Football League's main attraction, with a look at the main arena, press level, quadrant rooms, terrace level and box suites. $5.

The Presbytere (751 Chartres, 568-6968). Next to the St. Louis Cathedral, this old building houses permanent and changing exhibits of Louisiana culture and history.

Near New Orleans

Biloxi, Mississippi. Following an eighty-five mile drive east on Interstate 10, you will find pure white sand beach pleasure along the Gulf of Mexico.

Jean Lafitte National Historical Park and Preserve (589-2330). A 40-minute drive from the Quarter. Many of the park's trails are on elevated boardwalks, and will carry you over the saturated ground of swamp and marsh. Free.

Jean Lafitte Swamp Tours. In the summer, you are sure to see alligators and snapping turtles, and, possibly, wild boars. In the winter, it is a nice boat ride with an occasional glimpse of blue herons or snowy egrets. Both are educational trips into Louisiana's swamp culture. $20. Afterward, drive another ten miles to the town of Lafitte for a home cooked Cajun meal at **Boutte's** restaurant (689-7978). $4-15.

River Road Plantations (Take I-30 to Highway 48, 869-9752). For a self-guided tour of the cotton country giants, drive along the east or west banks of the Mississippi River north of New Orleans. Maps can be picked up at the Jackson Square tourist information kiosk.

KEEP FIT-RECREATION

Because of its proximity to swamps, a murky Lake Ponchartrain, and a Mississippi River that is off limits to recreationalists because of its international port industry, New Orleans is not the place to go to raise your anaerobic threshold. About the biggest workout you will get is walking around the French Quarter, and pumping libations instead of weights. Then again, there is always **City Park,** a 1500-acre tract near Lake Ponchartrain with four 18-hole golf courses, a 100-tee double-decker lighted driving range, 39 tennis courts, boat and bike rentals, and fishing and horse stables.

Bayou Women's Tennis Club (482-4807). An active social and athletic group. Call for a newsletter.

Frontrunners (947-1081). Meets Saturday mornings, 9 a.m., at the bench by the pond in Audubon Park along St. Charles Avenue.

EAT

Fine Dining

Commander's Palace (1403 Washington Ave., in Uptown, 899-8221). It is not only the impeccable Cajun and Creole cuisine, but the ambiance, as well, that consistently ranks the Palace as one of the best restaurants in America. The weekend brunches are equally as wonderful. Lunch, $12-24; dinner, $35-55.

Ralph & Kacoo's (519 Toulouse St., 522-5226). These people cook alligator meat to tender, juicy perfection. Or try the turtle soup or ostrich steak. And if you aren't so adventurous, stick with the boiled shrimp served with hush puppies. Whatever you order, it will be memorable. $6-20.

Feelings Café (2600 Chartres, 945-2222). Reservations are recommended in this more formal and pricey café, though the chipped plaster walls and antique mirror collection will seem a little ... off. Try the trout moutarde for Sunday brunch. And the peanut butter pie is to die for. Very gay friendly. $10-25.

K-Paul's Louisiana Kitchen (416 Chartres St., 524-7394). A purely Cajun cuisine with "blackened" everything from the famous Chef Paul Prudhomme's kitchen. Sit upstairs to mix with the locals. Otherwise, be prepared to wait for a table for a long, long time. $15-45.

Casual Dining

Buffa's (1001 Esplanade, 945-9373). With its spacious neighborhood pub atmosphere, it's a great place for sandwiches, soups and plate lunches. Or enjoy the daily special of southern fried veal cutlet or smothered chicken. Very gay friendly. $4-12.

Café Sbisa (1011 Decatur St., 522-5565). Seafood, steaks, French Creole food and Sunday brunch. Kitchen favorites include the baked filet of red fish with crawfish stuffing and the barbecued shrimp. Interesting artwork. Gay friendly. $13-20.

Clover Grill (900 Bourbon St., 523-0904). 1950s-style 24-hour diner in the heart of the gay area in the French Quarter. Very gay friendly. $3-9.

Hula Mae's Tropic Wash and Beach Cafe (838 Rampart St., 522-1336). In New Orleans, even doing the laundry becomes a culinary event. The cafe serves delicious po' boy sandwiches, soups and salads. And you can either do your laundry while you dine, or Hula Mae will pick up your dirty clothes from your hotel and return them in a couple of hours. Call for the free shuttle. Lesbian friendly. $3-6.

La Péniche (1940 Dauphine, 943-1460). A gay friendly, 24-hour hang-out. Quite popular the morning after a night at the bars. $3-8.

Napoleon House Bar and Cafe (500 Chartres St., 524-9752). The old-world ambiance of this corner cafe is a good place to begin your exploration of the French Quarter. Place yourself at a comfortable courtyard table, order a warm Italian muffuletta dressed with olive sauce, and a lemon-lime drink, and relax. $10-25.

Petunia's (817 St. Louis, 522-6440). A lovely, lesbian-owned crêperie with pink and green decor. For breakfast, try the "St. Peter" made with asparagus, cheddar, chicken and a perfect hollandaise sauce. If you can, sit at the two-top in front of the cozy coal-burning fireplace. $6-25.

Reality Grill (534 Frenchmen St., 945-2040). A delicious find on the second floor of a Faubourg-Marigny building. Giant French doors open into spacious dining rooms. A good bet is the pork tenderloin sandwich marinated in Tiger Sauce and dressed with All Fruit Chutney. Cash or check only. $6-14.

Vera Cruz (1141 Decatur, 561-8081). On Thursday nights, when Margaritas are two for the price of one, it seems like every gay person in town is packed into this place; food, often innovative and intriguing, frequently sizzles. Yummy fajitas. Large, crowded bar. Good place to nurse a few drinks. $7-16.

Coffeehouses

Café du Monde (1039 Decatur St., 800/772-2927). World famous *beignets* and café au laits — basically, the only items on the menu. Check out the efficient 1950s-style production line. $1-5.

Café Marigny (1913 Royal St., 945-4572). Known as *the* gay and lesbian coffeehouse. Fabulous menu of soups, salads, sandwiches and bagels, as well as a complete coffee bar and desserts. $1-10.

Bakeries

La Marquise Pastry Shop (625 Chartres St., 524-0420). An authentic French pastry shop with a beautiful courtyard through the back door.

NEW ORLEANS

♪ PLAY-MEET

Bars

Charlene's (940 Elysian Fields, 945-9328). Almost cafe-style with booths and country-ish decor, this women-only bar is an inviting place to hang out and talk to local women.

Donna's (800 N. Rampart, 596-6914). A bar with its own brass band across from the Louis Armstrong Park, and next door to the Lesbian and Gay Community Center.

Pat O'Briens (718 St. Peter, 525-4823). One of the best-known tourist night spots, and home to the popular Hurricane cocktail and Dixie beer. Open until 4 a.m.

Snug Harbor (626 Frenchmen St., 949-0696). Live jazz every night. In the past, such jazz greats as Ellis Marsalis and Charmaine Neville have performed here. Restaurant and bar open daily at 5 p.m.

Nightclub

Rubyfruit Jungle (640 Frenchmen, 947-4000). A high-energy lesbian and gay dance bar. Thursday nights at 10 p.m. offer specially priced cigars and cognacs. Owned by women.

Piano Bar

Feelings Cafe (2600 Chartres, 945-2222). The courtyard piano bar is a sweet place to start your vacation. Very lesbian friendly.

💰 SHOP

General Shopping

Magazine Street (from Canal Street to the Audubon Zoo). Some of the city's best restaurants and most interesting retail shops, art galleries and antique shops can be found here. Accessible by bus from

83

Canal Street, or from the St. Charles Streetcar, which runs parallel to Magazine Street.

River Walk Marketplace (522-1555). More than 140 unique and not-so-unique shops are a short walk from the French Quarter.

The Witches Closet (521 St. Philip, 593-9222). Owned by bona fide witches. Good luck charms, ritual altars, hexes removed, talismans, candles, sacred relics, voodoo dolls and occult jewelry.

Food Markets

French Market (1008 N. Peters St., 522-2621). The country's oldest continuously operated public market.

Matassa's Market (841 Iberville, 593-9050). The French Quarter's largest grocery, with a sit-down or take-out deli.

Quartermaster (1100 Bourbon, 529-1416). A grocery with wine and take-out sandwiches in the gay hub.

Pride Shopping

Alligator News and Books/Gay Mart (808 N. Rampart, 523-6005). Freedom rings, rainbow flags, decals and T-shirts. Located near the gay and lesbian community center.

Alternative Cards and Gifts (907 Bourbon St., 524-5222). Low-profile store with a lot of gay and lesbian stuff: cards, clothes and gifts. It's also convenient for photo finishing.

Postmark New Orleans (631 Toulouse, 529-2052). The best selection of greeting cards, and eclectic gifts and accessories for the home and bath. Look for the bubbles out front. Gay-owned.

Bookstores

Faubourg-Marigny Bookstore (600 Frenchmen St., 943-9875). The South's oldest gay, lesbian and feminist bookstore — you can tell by the creaky, warped wood floor — but the inventory is cutting edge.

Bookstar (411 N. Peters, 523-6411). In the Quarter, a mainstream bookstore with gay and lesbian titles and periodicals.

Moore Magic (1212 Royal St., 838-7918). A women's spirituality bookstore, full of literature, incense, herbs, oils and Tarot cards. Spiritual readings also available.

KIDS' STUFF

Audubon Zoo (6500 Magazine St., 861-2537). One of the best zoos in the country, especially known for its swamp exhibits. Plan to make a day of it. Adults, $7.50; children, $3.50.

Aquarium of the Americas (1 Canal St., 581-4629). Adults, $10; children, $5. Fairly new to the tourist scene, with presentations, animal feedings and shows daily. Commute between the Aquarium and the Zoo on the John James Audubon Riverboat for an extra $10 round trip.

SPIRITUAL

Grace Fellowship (3151 Dauphine, 944-9836).

Vieux Carre MCC (1128 St. Roch, 945-5390).

First Unitarian Church Gay & Lesbian Task Force (5212 S. Claiborne Ave., 822-3278).

Jewish Gay & Lesbian Alliance (525-8286).

Joie de Vivre MCC (330 E. Chimes, 383-0450).

RESOURCES

General Information

New Orleans Visitor's Bureau (529 St. Ann in Jackson Square, 566-5006).

Destination New Orleans (www.neworleans.net). Complete calendar of events and travel information.

Lesbian and Gay Community Center (816 N. Rampart St., 522-1103). Check the listings in *Impact* for art show openings and meetings hosted at the center.

Women's Music Collective (838-7918).
Womyn of Color (488-5708).

Media

Impact (944-6722, www.impactnews.com). Bi-weekly gay and lesbian news and entertainment magazine.

Offbeat (522-5533, www.neosoft.com/~offbeat). Covers the local music scene.

The Weekly Guide (522-4300). Pick up a copy at Café Marigny for listings of gay events. Women's listings are a bit slim.

Women's Healthy Pages (1501 Canal St., Room 710, 599-2308). A resource guide sponsored by the Tulane University Medical Center for Women's Health.

New York, New York

area code 212

WHAT TO EXPECT

So many women, and so little vacation time — it's the sentiment of many traveling lesbians as they depart New York City. There are a lot of women in New York — enough to fill all of the Denver metro area and still have some left over. And the majority of them are crammed onto the endearing island of Manhattan. There is no place else like it in the world. The mile-after-mile skyscrapers, ethnic neighborhoods, the spaghetti-configured subway system ... all make for a stimulating vacation filled with glorious babe-watching and urban exploration. Give yourself plenty of time to indulge in all of it.

A vacation in (Wo)Manhattan is similar to a non-stop caffeine buzz, the kind you last experienced when, from the moment you walked off the plane, you decided to try out all the coffeehouses in Seattle. All of your senses are on overdrive, even when you don't want them to be. You bounce out of bed every morning knowing that you are going to miss something if you sleep any longer. Hey, you want those bagels as fresh as they come, and you want to read the *New York Times* like every other New Yorker. Then, each day there are a million places to visit: Chinatown, the SoHo galleries and its sprightly shops, the Lower East Side Jewish neighborhood and delis, art museums, and, of course, gay-infested Chelsea and Greenwich Village. Or maybe the day has been set aside to "do" the Fifth Avenue-Central Park district, smothering yourself in the decadence of glamorous department stores, restaurants and one-of-a-kind boutiques. Don't forget, Central Park also beckons for an afternoon of picnicking, visiting the Metropolitan Museum of Art, renting in-line skates and, if it's winter, ice skating.

Of course, you will want to schedule a day or two in the lesbian-populated Brooklyn neighborhood of Park Slope — where, some claim, women are nesting and raising families. So be it. The "Slope" is also home for many single women, as well as the Lesbian Herstory Archives, which is one of the largest collections of lesbian-oriented print material. To get there, take the "F" subway from Manhattan to the Park Slope Seventh Avenue station, and from there, leading north on Seventh Avenue, you will find bookstores with the kind of interesting, feminist books you like to read, as well as intimate cafés, and the very best bagels. About a half-mile walk from the Seventh Avenue station you will find women gathered in the women-owned Rising Cafe and its neighbor, Beyond Words women's bookstore. It's the nucleus of lesbian social life in Manhattan's surrounding boroughs.

In the evenings, plan to be out all night because that's how long it takes to enjoy a cocktail and dinner, attend a reading at A Different Light bookstore or see a play, have a drink afterward, dance at one of the many electrifying women's nightclubs, and then hang out at a mellower bar, such as Rubyfruit Bar in Greenwich Village. The fun doesn't end there, though. You will wake up the next morning and do it all over again, even look forward to it. And, after returning home, you will still crave the dynamism of New York.

What To Bring

The 6 million women in the five-borough region wear anything and everything, from fur coats to out-of-sight pierced body parts, but there are a few common denominators. The first is a black French beret. Next, a pair of fat, black-rimmed glasses. If you bring a shoulder bag, make sure its color matches your coat. Always tuck an umbrella under your arm. And, finally, don't comb your hair.

Best Time To Visit

Between Thanksgiving and New Year's, during the holiday season.

NEW YORK

Getting There

It is cheaper to fly in and out of Newark International, in New Jersey, than JFK or La Guardia airports. From Newark International, **New Jersey Transit** (800/772-2222) buses depart for New York's Port Authority Bus Terminal at Eighth Avenue and 42nd Street every 15 minutes, 24 hours a day. Round-trip bus fare is $12.

Getting Around

Don't rent a car in New York. City politicians constantly come up with ludicrous reasons to write tickets: You made a left turn off of Fifth Avenue in February, or you honked the horn on 59th Street between Second and Third Avenues at 3:15 p.m. You will also spend $50 a day to keep it parked in a secured lot, only to find that you actually didn't need the car to begin with. Manhattan is a walker's delight with its mandatory window shopping and people watching. Also, subways, at $1.50 per ride, are relatively reliable (718/330-1234). And there is always a cab ride — the fastest, that is if it's not rush hour, and most thrilling way to cross town — beginning at $2.

STAY

Manhattan B&B Reservation Center (977-3512). Gay-owned, city-wide reservation system for hosted and unhosted rooms and apartments. $60-140.

NYC Apartment Swap Service (627-8612). A lesbian- and gay-oriented swapping program. They specialize in short-term sublets and long-term apartment shares.

Hotels

Chelsea Pines Inn (317 W. 14th St., 929-1023). A gay-owned hotel in the middle of the gay district, Chelsea. Lots of men around, and the rooms are nice. Each has a sitting area with couches and chairs. A Continental breakfast is included. $75-100.

Gramercy Park Hotel (21st St. and Lexington Ave., 800/221-

4083). Across the street from the city's only privately owned park and near the East Village, the hotel attracts cultural elites. Guests can use the hotel's key to the gated park. Funky digs, by all means. $135-180.

Hotel Washington Square (103 Waverly Pl., 777-9515). The rooms are a bit small, but, then again, being in the heart of the West Village means hotel time will be minimal with everything that's to be explored outside. Comfortable and clean. $85-140.

Guest Houses

East Village B&B (244 E. Seventh St. #6, 260-1865 or 473-0022). Manhattan's only lesbian-owned accommodation. Make reservations a year in advance, though, because the place fills up fast. Kids and pets are welcome. Two rooms — a single and a double — $50-75.

SEE-DO

In and Around New York

Angelika Film Center (995-2000). Often shows lesbian-related films.

Broadway, Off-Broadway and Off-Off-Broadway. Professional theater at its best. Show tickets are available at **TKTS** (47th St. and Broadway or the World Trade Center). Cash only.

Central Park. The great urban wilderness is not as dangerous as it is made out to be. Manhattanites escape to the park for solitude and recreation: cycling, in-line skating, ice skating, picnicking and babe watching. And the park also includes the **Metropolitan Museum of Art** (Fifth Ave. and 82nd St., 535-7710), **American Museum of Natural History** (79th St. and Central Park West, 769-5100), and **Central Park Zoo and Wildlife Center** (Fifth Ave. and 64th St., 861-6030).

Chinatown (South of the East Village). Characteristic of New York City's thriving street life, Chinatown is abuzz 'round the clock. Spend a day here in knickknack stores, herb shops, and among fish and vegetable venders.

Chinese Information and Culture Center (1230 Ave. of the

NEW YORK

Americas, 373-1800). Promotes an understanding of Chinese culture with a research library, classes, exhibits, films and performances.

Circle Line Sightseeing (Pier 83 at W. 42nd St. and the Hudson River, 563-3200). The Circle Line boat makes its trip around the island of Manhattan, and should be first on your list of things to do. The nighttime, two-hour tour is spectacular. Bring binoculars.

Empire State Building Observatories (350 Fifth Ave., 736-3100). On a clear day, check out this fantastic view of the urban jungle, all five boroughs and New Jersey. $4.50.

International Center of Photography (1130 Fifth Ave, at 94th St., 860-1777). The city's only museum devoted exclusively to photography, with permanent exhibits and featured artists. $4.

Jewish Museum (1109 Fifth Ave., 423-3200). Devoted to Jewish art and culture, ancient and modern. $7.

Kramer's Reality Tour (Pulse Theatre, 432, W. 42nd St., 268-5525). The inspirational character for *Seinfeld*'s Cosmo Kramer, Michael Richards, is now a tour guide for the pricey ride past notable *Seinfeld* plot spots in Manhattan — and, yes, the Soup Nazi is along the way. $37.50.

Museum of Modern Art (11 W. 53rd St., 708-9480). The building itself is lackluster, given that inside are some of the world's greatest art collections. Plan to attend any special exhibits early in the morning, or stand in line for a couple of hours. Thursday evenings are free.

New York Stock Exchange (20 Broad St., 656-5168). You've read about it in the newspapers, now see it live from a third floor viewing room. Admission is free, but tickets are limited, beginning at 9 a.m.

KEEP FIT-RECREATION

Chelsea Piers Sports Complex (Pier 62 at 23rd St. on the Hudson River, 336-6000). Plan on spending a day here. Women galore. Check out the six-story driving range, which is lighted at night against a backdrop of the New Jersey skyline. $31 per day, and bring a lock for a locker.

Frontrunners (724-9700, www.tiac.net/users/kaz/frny). Weekly

Saturday morning run meets at 10 a.m. at the Daniel Webster statue in Central Park, at West 72nd St. and West Park Drive. Afterward, join the group for socializing, coffee and bagels.

Women About (642-5257). An adventure social club for women that sheds light on the many definitions of "adventure." In addition to exploring the wilds, the group also tours Wall Street buildings, brunches in Chelsea, and has high tea in elite Manhattan hotels.

EAT

Fine Dining

Claire Restaurant (156 Seventh Ave., 255-1955). Every waiter is gay in this upscale lesbian hangout. Fresh fish and key lime pie are regular favorites. $6-20.

Indigo (142 W. 10th St., 691-7757). The award-winning chef has been around the block a few times and is tuned in to exquisite food. The wild mushroom strudel appetizer is a taste bud tease. After that, go for the feta cheese and roasted red pepper ravioli. Open for dinner only. $18-28.

Casual Dining

2nd Avenue Kosher Deli (156 Second Ave., 677-0606). This Jewish restaurant dishes up a wonderful bowl of matzo ball soup. Expect pickles on the table in the place of chips or bread. $3-15.

Angelica Kitchen (300 E. 12th St., 228-2909). A lovely vegetarian diner in the East Village. The "Daily Lunch Deal" is a nutritious bargain: cornbread smeared with miso dressing, a delicious sweet potato and carrot soup — or whatever the soup of the day is — and a house salad for $7. Lesbian friendly. $4-15.

Galaxy (15 Irving Place, 777-3631). Lesbian chef Debbie Stanton concocts meals that are out of this world, as is the decor of sparkling ceiling stars, halogen lighting and chrome accents. The Asian marinated duck confit, and wonton noodles in ginger lemongrass are earth-

NEW YORK

shattering. $8-16.

Les Deux Gamins (170 Waverly Pl., 807-7357). A leisurely and inviting place for long morning stays. Homemade preserves and thick, strong coffee. $3-10.

Regional Thai Taste (208 Seventh Ave., 807-9872). Heavily — or is that heavenly? — gay atmosphere. The traditional Pad Thai is spectacular, served with shrimp, chicken, peanuts, tofu, sprouts and lime. $4-15.

Rubyfruit Bar and Grill (531 Hudson St., 929-3343). A cozy, unpretentious diner downstairs, and a mellow lesbian bar upstairs. All the attention has been focused on creating unforgettable fare such as tender sirloins, lightly grilled salmon and free-range roasted chicken. $12-25.

Village Natural (46 Greenwich Ave., 727-0568). A popular vegetarian cafe where the gay crowd hangs out after meetings or movies at the Community Center. $2-10.

Coffeehouses

A Different Bite Cafe (151 W. 19th St., 989-4850). Located inside A Different Light Bookstore, it's a primo babe-watching spot. Serves light sandwiches as well. $2-6.

Big Cup (228 Eighth Ave., 206-0059). A Chelsea neighborhood coffeehouse with an upbeat atmosphere. Popular with the lesbian crowd. $2-7.

Decadence

Rumpelmayer's (50 Central Park South, in the St. Moritz Hotel, 755-5800). If you indulge in only one thing while in the uptown area, order a hot chocolate here. It's served with a giant bowl of whipped cream or marshmallows. Across the street from the south end of Central Park

The City Bakery (22 E. 17th St., 366-1414). Try the cranberry, almond and caramel tart — that is, indeed, tart — or the buttery, chocolatey Milky Way tart. $4.

GAY USA

♪ PLAY-MEET

Bars

Crazy Nanny's (21 Seventh Ave. S., 366-6312). Dance club and bar, with working-class women. The only place in New York where women can dance seven nights a week.
Cubbyhole (281 W. 12th St., 243-9041). Casual West Village neighborhood bar for lesbians. You can actually hear women speak above the music.
Henrietta Hudson (438 Hudson St., 924-3347). A laid-back women's bar. The kind of old-fashioned neighborhood bar where it's a pleasure to hang out and chat. Live music on Sundays.
Meow Mix (269 E. Houston, 254-1434). Artsy, Bohemian lesbian bar. A lot of younger Brooklyn babes frequent the joint. A good place to go for a casual game of pool.
Rubyfruit Bar (531 Hudson St., 929-3343). Saggy couches, but a down-to-Earth women's bar.

Dance Clubs

Bar d'O (29 Bedford, 627-1580). Sexy lesbian dancers in a lounge setting.
Kitty Glitter (266 E. 10th St., 677-1717). Lounge, light food selections. Mostly lesbians on Sunday nights. Pool shark chicks and glamour girls.
Clit Club (432 W. 14th St., 529-3300). The hottest thing since sliced bread. Attracts a diverse group of women every Friday night for a true rendition of a gay-la.
Club Casanova (99 Avenue B, 674-7957). Sunday night lesbian dance club. Begins at 10 p.m.
Her/She Bar (229 W. 28th St., 631-1102). Two floors of non-stop women's dancing on Friday nights.
Lesbian and Gay Dance (620-7310). On the second and fourth Saturday of each month, the Lesbian and Gay Community Center

NEW YORK

sponsors this fun get-together.

She-Bang (504 W. 16th St., 631-1102). A traveling Saturday night women's DJ party; drag king shows.

Shescape (686-5665). Hot dance parties held at various bars throughout the city. Call for listings.

WOW! (248 W. 14th St. at 8th Ave., 631-1102). World of women. Bar with three DJs and two floors on Wednesdays. Cabaret every Friday night.

Piano Bar

Julie's (204 E. 58th St., 688-1294). An uptown, upscale setting for the professional crowd. Usually, classy women drop by before crossing the Queens Bridge and heading home for the evening.

SHOP

General Shopping

Gallery Eclectic (43 Greenwich Ave., 924-4314). Lesbian-owned jewelry store.

P. Chanin (152 Eighth Ave., 924-5359). Lesbian-owned boutique on the gayest street in New York: Chelsea's Eighth Avenue.

Patricia Field (10 E. Eighth St., 254-1699). One-stop-shop for bold fashion statements. Lesbian owned.

Le Page Gallery (72 Thompson St., 966-2646). Lesbian artist and designer Cece Le Page specializes in modern luxuries for the home, often sculpting in acrylic: vases and trays, soap dishes, and swirling acrylic candlesticks.

Food Markets

Chocolate, fruit and wine can be found on every street corner. For more exotic groceries, consider these places:

Caviarteria (502 Park Ave., 759-7410). Caviar and foie gras.

Greenwich Village Fish Company (265 Bleeker St., 929-8042). Oysters and fresh seafood.

D'Agostino's (800/275-4324). Not an exotic grocery, but the city's main chain. There are more than 30 supermarkets scattered around Manhattan.

Whole Foods (117 Prince St., 982-1000). Healthy fare in SoHo, near the West Village.

Bookstores

A Different Light (151 W. 19th St., 989-2158, www.adlbooks.com). Manhattan's largest community shopping spot, includes books, CDs, T-shirts, a busy coffee shop, and a huge selection of gay- and lesbian-related books. Open mike is Saturday nights in the basement.

Creative Visions (548 Hudson St., 645-7573). Bookstore, cafe and performance space for the gay community.

Oscar Wilde Memorial Books (15 Christopher St., 255-8097). The world's first gay and lesbian bookshop in the heart of Greenwich Village, founded in 1967.

Three Lives (154 W. 10th St., 741-2069). Specializes in women's literature and frequently hosts readings by authors such as Rita Mae Brown. Lesbian-owned.

🐘 KIDS' STUFF

Coney Island Amusement Park (718/266-1234). Aquarium, Astroland Amusement Park, rides, games, wide open beach and the famous boardwalk.

Statue of Liberty (363-3200). Climb to the top for stunning views of the harbor. Adults, $7; children, $3.

American Museum of Natural History (Central Park West at 79th St., 769-5100). Mammoths, mastodons and saber-toothed cats in new halls of fossil mammals; also dinosaurs, meteorites and IMAX films.

Children's Museum of Manhattan (The Tisch Bldg., 212 W. 83rd

NEW YORK

St., 721-1234). Special hands-on exhibits and programs.
Sony Wonder Technology Center (550 Madison Ave., 833-8100). Visitors can help design the video games and techno-tools of the future.

SPIRITUAL

Axios Eastern and Orthodox Christians (718/229-0217). Gay and lesbian Armenians, Greeks and Russians meet at the Lesbian and Gay Community Center on second Friday of each month.
Christian Science Group (532-8379). Meets at the Lesbian and Gay Community Center on Thursday evenings.
Congregation Beth Simchat Torah (57 Bethune St., 929-9498). Jewish gays and lesbians meet for Friday evening service.
Dignity-New York (218 W. 11th St., 866-8047). Lesbian, gay and bisexual Roman Catholics meet for Sunday evening mass at St. John's Episcopal Church.
New York MCC (446 W. 36th St., between Eighth and Ninth Avenues, 242-1212). Services are on Sunday mornings.
Stephen Wise Free Synagogue (30 W. 68th St., 877-4050). Synagogue for Jewish lesbians and gay men.
Gay and Lesbian Buddhists-Maitri Dorje (619-4099). Meets weekly for worship.

RESOURCES

General Information

New York Convention and Visitors Bureau (2 Columbus Circle, 397-8222 or 800/NYC-VISIT).
Cultural Listings (765-ARTS). Free 24-hour hotline of upcoming events: theater, music, museums and dance.
African Ancestral Lesbians United for Societal Change (620-7310). Meets at the Center on Thursday evenings.
Bisexual Network (459-4784). Discussion groups and socials.

Butch-Femme Society (388-2736). Social group.
Las Buenas Amigas (633-2820). Group for Latina lesbians.
Lesbian and Gay Community Services Center (208 W. 13th St., off Seventh Ave., 620-7310, www.gaycenter.org). The grandmother of them all, the center publishes a monthly, four-page schedule of events using minuscule type.
Lesbian Switchboard (741-2610). Referrals and counseling.
SAL (718/630-9505). Social Activities for Lesbians sponsors meetings, support groups, birthday parties, outings and classes. Call ahead for a newsletter.

Media

HX for Her (627-5280, www.hx.com). Bills itself as the "party paper." Flip the pages to the "Dyke Dish" column for local gossip.
Clique (718/652-1928). A biweekly, somewhat racy women's magazine that is heavy on bar listings and personals.
LGNY (691-1100, www.gravity.fly.net/~lgny). A gay and lesbian bi-weekly with a political bent.
Time Out New York (460-8744, www.timeoutny.com). Complete critical listings in magazine form of every cultural event in the city.
Out-FM (279-0707). On WBAI-99.5 FM, Sundays, 6:30-7:30 p.m.

Festivals

Gay Pride. Traditionally, it takes place the last weekend in June. Call the Community Center (620-7310) for details.
Chinese New Year Parade. January or February, depending on the Chinese calendar. Call the Chinese Culture Center for information (373-1800).
New York Marathon. Annually in November. Call Frontrunners (724-9700).

NEW YORK

PARK SLOPE, BROOKLYN (Area Code 718)

STAY

Bed & Breakfast on the Park (113 Prospect Park West, 499-6115). If you don't stay in NYC, you can, at least, look at its amazing skyline from this splendid Victorian house. Or look the opposite direction toward Prospect Park and women's softball games. Woman-owned. $100-250.

SEE-DO

Lesbian Herstory Archives (484 14th St., 768-3953). A huge collection of lesbian writings. Call ahead for an appointment.

EAT

Charlie's (Seventh Ave. and President St., 783-0747). The deli is about 3-feet wide and sells just about everything imaginable. Great bagels. $1-10.

Henrietta's (787 Union St., 622-2924). Delicious vegetarian menu. The fried tempeh with vegetables and greens is tasty, as is the fresh carrot juice. $3-8.

Koko Bar (59 Lafayette Ave., 243-9040). Cyber cafe with a nice sandwich menu. Lesbian-owned. $2-6.

Rising Cafe (186 Fifth Ave. at Sackette St., 789-6340). The menu consists of pastries and two choices of soups, as well as coffees, beer and wine. The dimly lit room makes for a nice place to hang out. Toys for kids. Lesbian-owned. $2-5.

PLAY-MEET

Sanctuary (444 Seventh Ave., 832-9800). A new, gay, dance bar. Small, attractive place. Lesbian friendly.

Carry Nation (363 Fifth Ave., 788-0924). More traditional gay and lesbian neighborhood bar with a pool table.

One Hot Spot (1 Front St., 852-0139). A gay and lesbian bar in Brooklyn, but not actually in Park Slope.

Spectrum Disco (802 64th St., 238-8213). Gay friendly bar.

SHOP

Food Market

Back to the Land (142 Seventh Ave., 768-5654). Complete natural foods store.

Bookstore

Beyond Words (184 Fifth Ave., 857-0010). A small, lesbian-owned bookstore with a good selection of women's books, local newspapers and magazines. Readings feature local lesbian writers.

San Francisco, California

area code 415

WHAT TO EXPECT

The word "beautiful" comes to mind when thinking about San Francisco — trite as it may be — because everything in the city seems to be taken out of a picture book, from antique cable cars to seafood mongers on Fisherman's Wharf. Look around! There are intricately painted Queen Anne and Victorian row houses, and the subway system — BART — is spic-and-span compared to other cities'. Even the women are gorgeous: slender, tall, well-dressed, killer hair. It's too bad that many of them are actually men.

When you think about it, San Francisco has always attracted the kinder, gentler qualities in people, which, perhaps, accounts for the large population of peace activists. Remember the 1966 "Summer of Love" mascots — who left in their wake "love burgers," "flower power" and the peace symbol? It's no wonder that San Francisco has emerged as one of the more liberal North American cities, having a renowned attitude of tolerance that serves as a metaphorical welcome mat for unorthodox lifestyles. Consequently, its streets are anything but straight and narrow.

Speculation has it that at least 100,000 of San Francisco's 750,000 residents are gay, but nobody has ever tried to figure out how many of those people are lesbians. But visit the Castro's neighboring Bernal Heights and the Mission District's Valencia Street and it will be obvious that it is not just men who account for an estimated 25-percent of the city's gay votes. A visit to the Castro District, even if it's for the first time, will bring goose bumps and a great sense of community. After all, the Castro is home to many "firsts" for the gay movement, as well as the largest contingent of "Dykes on Bikes" any gay pride parade has ever known. Other "firsts" include the election of Harvey Milk, who was the first elected city-official to be an openly gay man; Twin Peaks bar at the corner of Castro and Market Streets, which was the first gay bar in the world to have street-side windows; and San Francisco, which was the first American city to enact an anti-discrimination law for homosexuals.

As for gay women, San Francisco has always been in the limelight of social and political change. In 1955, Del Martin and Phyllis Lyon, a pair of lesbian lovers, moved to the Castro from Seattle, and wanted something to do besides frequent bars, of which there weren't many at the time. The couple founded Daughters of Bilitis, and it became the first "out" lesbian organization in the country. By 1960, Daughters of Bilitis had sprouted regional chapters nationwide, and celebrated its first national convention, which, of course, took place in San Francisco. Now, in honor of these foremothers, the Lyon-Martin Women's Health Services Center, at 1748 Market Street, is the first, and only, city-funded lesbian memorial in the nation.

There have been other women's shrines, as well. When the feminist bookstore Old Wives' Tales, formerly on Valencia Street, went out of business in 1995, a soulful cry was heard throughout the land, as it left a gaping hole in independent women's book sellers, not to mention community centers. What was feared as a turn for the worst in the nation's most-watched lesbian land actually caused other feminist-oriented businesses to thrive. After all, a woman's gotta be able to spend her money and social time somewhere.

What To Bring

There is more of a "look" to San Francisco lesbians than a "wardrobe." Many women opt for shaved, buzzy haircuts, jeans and black, heavy boots, accompanied by heavy piercing. Others take the borderline chilly-to-warm weather seriously and wear tights and big down jackets, and not much more.

SAN FRANCISCO

Best Time To Visit

The holidays from late November through December are a fun time to be in San Francisco. Theater and music seasons are in full gear, Union Square ice rink is bustling and florists' shops overflow with fresh flowers. Although December to March is the wet season, sometimes, especially during a drought, the spring weather is pleasant with highs near 60 degrees.

As far as lesbian holidays go, one of the gay world's signature events — Pride Fest — takes place in San Francisco the last full week of June. The parade itself is like none other, as are the reams of events leading up to it.

Getting Around

After flying into San Francisco Airport, take the No. 7F Samstran bus to the downtown Transbay station for $2.50. From Oakland International Airport, take the **AirBART** bus ($2.00) to the **BART** station (992-2278), then catch the Daly City line to the Transbay Station in downtown San Francisco. Once at Transbay, transfer to the "F" streetcar, operated by **Muni** (673-6864), which runs the length of Market Street to Castro every 20 minutes and costs only $1. Muni passports, which include streetcars and buses, are available for one day ($6), three days ($10) and seven days ($15), and are good on every Muni vehicle, except cable cars.

STAY

Luxury

Juliana Hotel (590 Bush St., 392-2540). The hotel offers a mixture of French Provençal interiors, a cozy lobby with a wood-burning fireplace and fresh flowers, and an in-house Italian restaurant called Vinoteca. It is mostly staffed by women and borders Chinatown and the Financial District. $120-150.

Guest Houses

House O' Chicks (2162 15th St., 861-9849). The only lesbian-owned guest house in the Castro District. Rooms may have shrines to porn queen Annie Sprinkles, but consider it a continuation of the 1968 Summer of Love, which took place in the nearby Haight-Asbury area. There are no rules here, and the house is comfortable and clean, with complimentary use of the owner's kitchen, office computer, printer and fax machine. $50-100.

Mary Elizabeth Inn (1040 Bush St., 673-6768). Located on Nob Hill. A residence for women daily, weekly and monthly. Rates include most meals. $49.

SEE-DO

In and Around San Francisco

Alcatraz Island (546-2628). How can this island with a pretty name — alcatraz is the Spanish word for pelican — and a great location have such a grim history? A daily, ranger-led tour explores different aspects of the island, from Native American lore to military takeover. Board the Black & White Fleet on Pier 41, but call ahead of time for a reservation. Adults, $11; children 5-11, $5.75.

Phoebe Apperson Hearst Museum of Anthropology (Kroeber Hall, at Bancroft Way and College Ave., Berkeley, 510/642-3681). The Hearst matriarch is known for single-handedly raising the status of the University of California from a respectable state school to one of the pre-eminent universities along the west coast, especially focusing her funds on women's scholarships. The museum's exhibits often deal with women's culture.

Cable Cars (673-6864). A Victorian edict for San Francisco's original mass transportation system — invented in 1873 — prohibited women from hanging on the outside of the cars until a court order in 1964. It was viewed as unladylike. Now, the thrill of hanging costs $2.

Japantown (1750 Geary Blvd., 922-9300). Spend at least a day

SAN FRANCISCO

trying on authentic kimonos, eating sushi, and sipping green tea while shopping for hard-to-find-back-home kitchen utensils such as a sesame seed grinder. An afternoon at the Kabuki Hot Springs — a traditional Japanese bathhouse — is always a good idea. The communal facilities are reserved for women only on Wednesdays, Fridays and Sundays.

Osento (955 Valencia, 282-6333). The word "sento" in Japanese means "penny bath." Of course, social baths cost more than that now. Osento is a long-standing Valencia Street woman-owned and women-only business. Door fee is $8-13 for a hot tub and sauna; an eight-time tub card is $48; and a one-hour massage, hot tub and sauna is $45-65.

The Names Project (2362-A Market St., 863-1966). This is a solemn stop in the Castro-Market area, but an essential one. Anybody can visit the place where the AIDS memorial quilt began and look at photos of different exhibits in Washington, DC. But the primary focus of the visitor center is to offer all the materials needed to make a quilt square, which isn't really square. Blocks of the quilt measure 6 feet by 3 feet, the same size as a coffin. Fabric scraps, cutting tables, sewing machines and moral support are available free of charge. To view a particular panel, call the 310 Townsend Street warehouse in advance (882-5500).

Walking Tours. The following are a few gems from which to choose: **Cruising the Castro** (550-8110). Tour guide Trevor Hailey sits you down in front of the Eureka Valley Recreation Center before the tour begins and puts the gay and lesbian universe into focus, finally narrowing in on Castro. It is worth the four to five phone calls it takes to track her down and make a reservation; $30 includes brunch at Caffe Luna Piena. **Wok Wiz** (800/281-WALK) is an insider tour of Chinatown with a cruise through a noodle factory, and a delicious dim sum lunch; $35. **Mission District Mural Walks** (285-2287). Meets every Saturday, 1:30 p.m., at 348 Precita Ave., and doesn't view all of the 250 murals painted during the 1970s, but you will see a good number of them in San Francisco's oldest neighborhood; $4. Finally, there is the **Hunting Bargains** tour (892-1088), a daily shopping tour of the city's garment district's designer warehouses and showrooms. Half day and full day tours are available, if you can stand it. In the end, you will be better dressed, worn out, and considerably poorer.

Women's Building (3543 18th St., 431-1180). It is not often that you get goose bumps looking at a building. The four-story structure is painted in the famous Mission District mural fashion that took seven women artists three years to create. The Lapidge Street facade is a montage of women throughout history: Audre Lorde and her spirit, the Aztec goddess of the moon, 1993 Nobel Peace Prize recipient Guatemalan Rigoberta Menchu, and the Pliades star constellation, just to name a few. The 18th Street wall is anchored by an African American woman and an Ohlone native California woman, their hands draped with yards of fabric from around the world. The center itself hosts women's events and houses several women's groups.

Women's Philharmonic (330 Townsend St., 543-2297). A professional women's orchestra dedicated to performing the work of women composers. Its season runs from October to May.

Near San Francisco

Muir Woods National Monument (Mill Valley, 12 miles north of San Francisco on Highway 101, 388-2595). The only large stand of redwoods in the Bay Area, with some trees more than 3000 years old.

Point Reyes National Seashore (U.S. Hwy. 1, 38 miles north to Bear Valley Rd., 453-2100). The fifteen miles of pristine beaches do not offer any swimming, but strolling, bird watching, wading and meditating are highlights. The annual Labor Day sand castle-building contest on Drake's Beach is a heated competition between several San Francisco architectural firms.

KEEP FIT-RECREATION

Different Spokes (282-1647). A gay and lesbian bicycling group for the Bay Area. Call for a weekly schedule of road and mountain-bike rides.

Dyke Hackers (824-1453). Lesbian golf club holds regular outings and produces a monthly newsletter.

Wilderness Women (510/658-2196). The group has regular outings for hiking, bird watching, kayaking and skiing.

SAN FRANCISCO

Women's Training Center (2164 Market St., at Sanchez, 864-6835). A gym near Castro for both lesbians and straight women.

EAT

Fine Dining

Greens (in Fort Mason, at Marina Blvd. and Laguna, 771-6222). The ambiance of this upscale vegetarian restaurant cries out for some background piano music, or any music, for that matter. Still, the incredible food, such as pumpkin tart and warm cabbage salad, can be savored along with unspoiled views of the Golden Gate Bridge and the bay. $12-20.

Ma Tante Sumi (4243 18th St., 552-6663). One of the Castro District's most charming and intimate restaurants, offering superb cuisine that blends California with France and the Pacific. Dinner only. Call ahead for reservations. $20-30.

Casual Dining

The best tacquerias in town are in the 24th and Mission Street area. All of them are good, as bad food doesn't last long in the Mission District.

Bagdad Cafe (2295 Market St., 621-4434). All the food is prepared fresh on the premises with vegetarian meals. It is open twenty-four hours, and the lesbian wait staff is happy and good looking; the clientele is eclectic, casual and hungry. Lesbian-owned. $4-10.

Boogaloos (3296 22nd St. at Valencia, 824-3211). A good, gay friendly breakfast place. The temple of spuds is a good bet, as well as the polenta and eggs with chicken-apple sausage. $4-8.

Caffe Luna Piena (558 Castro St., 621-2566). A gay-owned Italian restaurant that serves exceptionally fresh fare. Be sure to sit out back on the terrace. $5-16.

Josie's Cabaret and Juice Joint (3583 16th St., 861-7933). A vegetarian cafe by day, and a gay and lesbian talent hot spot by night.

Events range from stand-up comedy to musicians and theater troupes. $4-7.

Rasoi (1037 Valencia St., 695-0599). Interesting decor of sponge stenciling. The northern Indian cuisine features murgh tikka masala — a creamy tomato sauce with fenugreek and a dash of brandy — among many other dishes steeped in cumin, coriander and cinnamon. $5-12.

Red Dora's Bearded Lady Cafe (485 14th St., 626-2805). A one-of-a-kind, small, lesbian-owned and frequented establishment, serving tasty vegetarian treats in a smoke- and alcohol-free zone. It's also a gallery and home to various lesbian performers. $4-12.

The Rooster (1101 Valencia at 22nd, 824-1222). The Italian decor fits in with the Valencia Street Renaissance mode, and the food is *delisioso*. Try the butternut squash ravioli. $12-15.

Ti-Couz (3108 16th St., 25-CREPE). A small, woman-owned Breton crêperie across from the Roxie Cinema, offering savory and sweet concoctions. All are excellent. $4-10.

Val 21 (995 Valencia at 21st, 821-6622). There is a large lesbian presence at this Valencia Street establishment, which features lime-ginger prawns with a pesto marinade, and arugula-goat cheese salad. $12-19.

East Bay

Brick Hut (2512 San Pablo, Berkeley, 510/486-1124). This lesbian-owned institution began as a collective back in the 1970s when there was a huge women's community in Berkeley. Today, the place continues to cook up a delicious breakfast, and oh, so many lesbians in one place. $5-8.

Caffka (4252 Piedmont Ave., Oakland, 653-1647). A woman-owned European-style cafe featuring delicious coffee drinks, Italian-style sandwiches and an array of desserts. $4-9.

Coffeehouses

Cafe Flore (2298 Market St., 621-8579). The place to be seen,

SAN FRANCISCO

this cafe is always buzzing with the hip gay crowd. Breakfast is served until 3 p.m. Lunch features inventive salads. And, of course, there is a full coffee bar. $5-9.

Just For You Bakery and Cafe (1453 18th St., 647-3033). Open for breakfast and lunch only, the Potrero Hill restaurant attracts a lesbian clientele. Lesbian-owned. $3-9.

♪ PLAY-MEET

Dance Clubs

Club Q (177 Townsend, 647-8258). "Mixtress" Page Hodel packs the women in here, and has for six years. The first Friday of every month at the massive Club Townsend.

Coco Club (139 Eighth St., 626-2337). The last Friday of every month anything goes at Coco Club: erotic readings, dancing, and sometimes a lesbian dating game, which is always interesting, whether you are participating or not.

Faster Pussycat (911 Folsom, hotline 561-9771). Every Sunday night at the Coco Club. Occasionally FP holds fund-raisers for places like the Black and Blue tattoo shop — next door to Red Dora's Bearded Lady Cafe — and features local women's bands. Call to get on the mailing list.

G-Spot (278 11th St., 337-4962). San Francisco's nerve center for lesbian night life every Saturday night. An exhilarating, giddy, go-go filled affair. You might qualify for a cover-charge discount if you show up dressed in only a brassiere.

Muffdive (527 Valencia St., 863-9328). This is the serious punker lesbo alternative night club every Sunday night at the Cassanova.

The Box (715 Harrison at Third St., 972-8087). Some of the finest funk, soul and high-energy dance music every Thursday evening in the old Dreamland space in Soma (South of Market). If you like dancing at a slower pace, try the small dance floor in front of the entrance that plays soul and hip hop. A great cross section of boys and girls, all having a blast.

Bars

The Cafe (2367 Market St., 861-3846). A fun, lesbian bar in the Castro with some men around. Located above **Gauntlet** (861-3846), a clit-piercing spot at Castro and Market. The Cafe has a dance floor, pool tables and a patio.

Twin Peaks Tavern (401 Castro St., 864-9470). Owned by two lesbians and opened in 1972, Twin Peaks was the first gay bar in the U.S. to have windows. The clientele is mostly men, but then again, it's on the corner of Castro and Market Streets.

Wild Side West (424 Cortland, 647-3099). A funky 30-year-old establishment in cozy Bernal Heights, making it the oldest lesbian bar in the city. Not only is it a good place to watch the television sports game of the week, but you can also sip from a drink on the back porch swing and shoot some pool on the pink-felt-covered table.

SHOP

General Shopping

Cliff's Variety (479 Castro St., 431-5365). Cliff's dime store was the first retailer on Castro Street to employ openly gay and lesbian people. Then, the store became a gay home depot, catering to the gay man and everything he might need to set up housekeeping. Today, it is one of the most popular stores in the area.

Good Vibrations (1210 Valencia, 974-8980). Known for its mail-order bedroom goodies. Once you actually wander inside the store, the happy clerks will make you feel at home. And because there will be a waiting line at the cashier, take time to gawk at the vintage vibrator exhibit — artifacts that were collected at garage sales. Woman-owned and operated. Also in Berkeley at 2504 San Pablo, 510/841-8987.

Haight Street (from Stanyan St. to Masonic Blvd.). In the 1960s one could shop for drugs in the area. Nowadays, there are unique stores, restaurants, night clubs, hip ice cream parlors, and vintage clothing shops that offer a melange of used 1960s and 70s fashions.

SAN FRANCISCO

Union Square (323 Geary St., 781-7880). The half-mile radius that is bound by Powell, Stockton, Geary and Post Streets downtown forms a gigantic shopping district that includes major department stores, small shops, theaters, restaurants and art galleries.

Food Markets

Harvest (2285 Market St., 626-0805). Not only does the Harvest have the best salad bar this side of the Mississippi, but anything organic, unusual and decadent can be found here, including cilantro tortillas and "Devil Girl" chocolate bars that are made by Northampton women.

Valencia Whole Foods (999 Valencia St., 285-0231). Organic produce, bulk foods, vitamins, natural cosmetics, deli foods, coffees, teas and herbs.

Secondhand Stores

Community Thrift (623 Valencia St., 861-4910). The store will make a donation to your favorite charity, such as the lesbian monthly newspaper "Dykespeak."

Pride Shopping

Wild Card (3979-B 17th St., 626-4449). The Castro's best and most extensive collection of greeting cards, gifts, novelty items, jewelry and posters.

Bookstores

A Different Light (489 Castro St., 431-0891, www.adlbooks.com). Part of the Los Angeles-New York chain, featuring an extensive selection of titles les-bi-gay titles.

Bernal Books (401 Cortland Ave., Bernal Heights, 551-0293). A woman-owned bookstore in the popular lesbian neighborhood that's two suburbs to the south of the Castro District. A good selection of cards, books, jewelry and music.

Boadecia's (398 Colusa Ave., Kensington, East Bay, 510/559-9184). A bookstore that is active in the women's community, Boadecia's offers readings, holiday de-stresser meetings, a stitch-and-bitch evening, and on-going book groups.

Mama Bears (6536 Telegraph, Oakland, East Bay, 510/428-9684). The East Bay institution was started in the 1970s when Oakland and Berkeley were the lesbian hot spots, and still carries some of its '70s flavor. Now there is a coffee shop, and a monthly newsletter for upcoming events.

Modern Times (888 Valencia, 2282-9246). This progressive bookstore took over as Valencia Street's anchor bookstore when San Francisco's only women's bookstore Old Wives Tales shut down in the winter of 1995. There is a dominant les-bi-gay section, and the clientele is heavily lesbian.

West Berkeley Women's Books (2514 San Pablo Ave., Berkeley, 510/204-9399). A relatively new East Bay feminist bookstore, located next door to the legendary Brick Hut.

KIDS' STUFF

Barbie Doll Hall of Fame (460 Waverly St., Palo Alto, 326-5841). The icon of our childhoods is presented in more than 16,000 versions in a little museum near Stanford University. Maybe on your way to a Stanford women's basketball game you can drop by.

Cartoon Art Museum (814 Mission St., 227-8666). Dedicated to original cartoon art in all its forms. It is also a great place to spark up childhood memories for us older kids.

Exploratorium (3601 Lyon-Marina Blvd., 561-0360). A world-famous interactive science museum with more than 650 "hands on" exhibits. Don't go by yourself, though; it is not as much fun.

International Children's Art Museum (World Trade Center, Suite 103, 772-9977). The museum's goal is to foster communication and understanding among the children of the world through the universal language of art.

SAN FRANCISCO

☼ SPIRITUAL

Congregation Sh'ar Z'hav (220 Danvers St., 861-6932). Jewish reform lesbian and gay congregation every Friday at 8:15 p.m.
Goddess-oriented Bisexual Women's Group (979-4023). Meets monthly.
Metropolitan Community Church (150 Eyreka St., 863-4434).
Most Holy Redeemer Parish (100 Diamond St., 863-6259). Located in the heart of the Castro, this is the church of preference for many Catholic homosexuals. The weekly Bingo games rock.
Saint Francis Lutheran Church (152 Church St., 621-2635). The church was recently excommunicated from the Evangelical Lutheran Church of America because the congregation ordained two out lesbians, who also happened to be very friendly with each other.

☏ RESOURCES

General Information

San Francisco Visitor's Bureau (391-2000).
Alameda Lesbian Potluck Society (510/522-8312). Holds monthly potlucks in the East Bay, but you don't have to be from the East Bay to attend.
Bi Women's Group (775-2620). Meets third Wednesday of every month for potlucks, parties, movies and outdoor activities.
Deaf Gay and Lesbian Center (TDD 255-0700).
Lesbian Clinic (2908 Ellsworth, Berkeley, 843-6194). Housed in the Berkeley Women's Health Collective, the facility offers health care for lesbians.
Lesbians over 50 (285-0239). A drop-in support-discussion group that meets periodically. Call ahead for topic of the week or month.
Rainbow Clinic (476-1777). Provides pediatric care for children of gay and lesbian parents. Call for appointment.

Media

Bay Times (227-0800, www.baytimes.com). With a woman publisher-editor, the premier San Francisco les-bi-gay biweekly newspaper covers the women's scene pretty well.

Bay Area Reporter (861-5019). A weekly newspaper aimed heavily at gay men, yet the staff has a sense of humor, as well as an in-depth view of the Castro area.

Dykespeak (282-0942). A small, sophisticated women's monthly. No cartoons, no horoscopes and great personals.

QTV (956-1284). Tuesdays on Viacom, channel 47, 7-8 p.m.

Q San Francisco (800/764-0324, http://qsanfrancisco.com). An informative bimonthly magazine that covers the city scene, and lists restaurants, bars and touristy things.

Seattle, Washington

area code 206

WHAT TO EXPECT

Despite its rain and an impressive range of shades of gray in the skies, Seattle remains a bright spot along the northwest coast — and should be included on every woman's list of favorite cities. For one thing, the air is clean. But what do you expect from constant rainfalls, and breezes off the Puget Sound? And when the sun *does* shine, it is incredibly blinding. In fact, statistics show that more sunglasses are sold per capita in Seattle than in any other city, which is not just because of the sun's brightness. One Seattleite confessed that she always misplaces her sunglasses during rainy days, and has to purchase new ones during the few-and-far-between sunny reprieves.

Consequently, Seattleites have turned to coffee as a means of warming their water-logged bodies. Not only are Seattle natives born with the inherent knowledge of how to froth the perfect cappuccino, they have invented the language of the entire coffee nation. Soon, coffee jargon as we know it — a "Why Bother?" or a "Buzz Cone" — will be reinvented by Seattle's Capitol Hill gay and lesbian community. Before we know it, we'll be ordering a "tall, skinny Martina with a white hat on a leash" — a large Scandinavian-blend topped with skimmed-milk foam, to go — or a "short K.D. latte." How about a "Gertrude Stein Gertrude Stein *sans* punctuation" — a double-black Americano? At this point, nobody in Capitol Hill blinks twice at such reverence.

Once you get over the shock of being in Latte Land, you will realize another of Seattle's greatest attributes: shopping. Before the Klondike Gold Rush of 1898, Seattle retailers, collectively, earned $300,000 in annual sales. Then, when the fever struck, and most gold diggers passed through Seattle on their way to Canada's Yukon, local merchants brought in more than $25 million in less than eight months, considerably revving up the competition for consumer dollars. Although not every lesbian lives to shop, there are some spectacular spots in the Emerald City. Today, the great shopping tradition continues with Nordstrom's, the Pike Place Market — home of the city's best produce, seafood and art — the colossal selection of outdoor gear stores, and the Broadway Market on Capitol Hill, all of which are lesbians' shopping preferences.

But what makes Seattle a really great lesbian city, besides its coffee and shopping, is how women take to the outdoors. Forget the rain, and slugs that find refuge in shoes. Forget the mud and dampness. As a tourist, you shouldn't let a little bit of gray sky stop you from exploring many of Seattle's parks, beaches and waterways. Volunteer Park, at 11th Avenue and Highland Drive, is where many women settle in for picnics, volleyball and the unlikely pastime of sunbathing. Also, Dyke-ki-ki Beach — named after Hawaii's Waikiki — along Lake Washington Drive just north of Yesler Way at Denny-Blaine Park, is a popular spot for lesbian swimming rendezvous. And Green Lake, situated near the lesbian-populated Wallingford neighborhood, is where many women have been seen walking dogs, playing with children, and in-line skating or jogging on the lake's surrounding pathways. Not to mention it's a good place to lounge in the grass, if it's dry, and people watch.

Inevitably, there is a special rapture shared by lesbians who are high on Seattle, which is something akin to a blend of caffeinated, artistic, wild energy in praise of sloppy weather and the outdoors. It all kind of percolates up through you. And when you place your feet on the Arthur Murray-like, bronze, dance footprints that are inlaid along Capitol Hill sidewalks — part of an art-in-public-places project — you can't help but raise your arms toward the gray, lovely, and probably wet skies. And you dance!

What To Bring
Short-sleeved cotton T-shirt under a hooded slicker, and sunglasses.

Best Time To Visit
According to Seattleites, July 26 is the one day of the year when it

SEATTLE

is fairly certain the sun will be out. In the words of comedian Jerry Seinfeld, "Seattle is a moisturizing pad disguised as a city."

Getting Around

Walking is the best way to explore the downtown area. The Metro Transit System (553-3000) offers free rides anywhere in downtown Seattle from 4 a.m. to 9 p.m. Beyond downtown, transit fares range from 85 cents to $1.60. Be sure to have a look inside the bus tunnel, where buses drive beneath the city. There, commissioned artwork decorates each station.

Washington State Ferries (464-6400, or 800/84-FERRY). Across the Puget Sound, ferries taxi passengers between Seattle, Vashon Island, Bremerton and Bainbridge Island. Ferries also travel as far north as Homer, Alaska. **The Victoria Clipper** (800/888-2535) operates passenger service between Seattle and Victoria, British Columbia.

STAY

Hotel

Capitol Hill Inn (1713 Belmont Ave, 323-1955). You can't be any closer to the heart of Capitol Hill's land o' lesbians than by staying in this lesbian-owned restored Queen Anne house. The rooms are comfortable and within walking distance of several lesbian hang-outs. Children and pets not permitted. Includes full breakfast. $85-165.

SEE-DO

In and Around Seattle

Alice B. Arts (1202 E. Pike, 32-ALICE). An eclectic celebration of queer theater. Performance calendar is erratic, so call ahead for a schedule.

Art Walks (367-6831). Visit galleries, watch people, eat dinner and have fun in Seattle's Pioneer Square on the first Thursday of each month.

Boeing Museum of Flight (9404 E. Marginal Way S., 764-5720). View films and 50 full-size aircraft, and learn about the men and women who pioneered the air-travel industry. Adults, $8; children, $4.

Discovery Park (386-4236). The largest urban wilderness area in Seattle; public beaches, ponds, woods with hiking trails, nesting eagles, and tons of activities for children.

Hiram Chittenden Locks (3015 NW 54 St., 783-7059). Watch how boats pass through the canal that locks in the fresh waters of Salmon Bay, Lake Union and Lake Washington, and locks out the salt water of Puget Sound. Underwater viewing of fish; botanical gardens.

Pike Place Market (Pike St. and First Ave., 682-7453). This is the heart and soul of the city. Nooks and crannies reveal unusual shops, bakeries, fresh produce and seafood stands, and stalls featuring the handiwork of local artisans.

Pioneer Square (a few blocks south of Pike Place Market). Built in 1889 after a fire destroyed many of the original downtown buildings, the restored brick buildings in Seattle's historic district now house shops, art galleries, restaurants, bookstores and nightclubs. After the fire, streets were raised as much as 35 feet, and a new city was built on top of the old one. On the **Underground Tour,** which begins at Doc Maynard's Public House (610 First Ave., 682-4646), visitors can walk along the subterranean streets and explore remains of the original city's old hotels, banks, shops and gambling dens.

Seattle Art Museum (100 University Ave., 654-3100). Internationally recognized for excellence in Asian, African, Native American and modern art of the Pacific Northwest. Look for the daunting "Hammering Man" sculpture out front. Adults, $6; children, $4.

Washington Park Arboretum (2300 Arboretum Dr. E., 543-8800). A compressed world of mountains, forests and rivers that celebrates Japanese botanical history. It is especially lovely in springtime.

Near Seattle

Mount Rainier National Park (100 miles southeast of Seattle on

SEATTLE

State Route 7, 706/569-2211). The two-hour drive takes you to Seattle's most imposing landmark — at 14,400 feet. The Park's guides conduct free tours of the area during August. Check the visitors' center for schedules.

Snoqualmie Falls (Off I-90, 30 minutes east of Seattle, 888-4440). These dramatic falls plunge 286 feet into a rocky gorge, which is 100 feet taller than Niagara Falls. Hiking trails lead to the base of the falls. While you are there, stop in at the **Snoqualmie Winery** for wine tasting, or a picnic on the beautiful grounds. Also, **Snoqualmie Pass** is a popular trailhead for hikers during dry days.

Nearby **Tacoma** is home to the **Tacoma Art Museum** (272-4258) and historic **Point Defiance Park, Zoo and Aquarium** (591-5335). In **Fireman's Park** (S. Eighth and "A" streets) stands one of the nation's tallest totem poles at 82 feet, carved from a single cedar by Alaskan natives.

KEEP FIT-RECREATION

Lesbian Orca Swim Club (325-3604). Meets on Monday and Wednesday, 7-8:30 p.m., at the Medgar Evers Pool, at 23rd and Cherry.

Womyn of Wheels (527-1852). Seattle-area lesbian bicycling group. Outings range from inner-city fun rides, to weekend tours of the Cascade mountains.

Frontrunners (322-DYKE). Meet at Green Lake, at 9 a.m., Saturday mornings. A breakfast social hour follows the run. The first Saturday of each month is Womyn's Run Day, in which women head off in their own direction and pace.

EAT

Fine Dining

Shuckers (at the Four Seasons Olympic Hotel, 411 University, 621-1984). This upscale eatery features at least seven varieties of local oysters, King crab and fresh, smoked salmon. A wonderful spot for a romantic dinner. $12-30.

The Painted Table (92 Madison St. at First, 624-3646). Dinners are what locals call "fusion-style" cooking — a combination of Thai, Japanese and Korean cuisine. Try the seared tuna. $10-25.

Casual Dining

Broadway New American Grill (314 Broadway E., 328-7000). The usual diner-pub fare with some surprises, such as the grilled chicken and brie cheese sandwich. Blue plate specials are available daily before 4 p.m., and breakfast is served any time. $4-13.

Cafe Septieme (214 Broadway E., 860-8858). The grilled polenta with poached eggs and black bean salsa makes for a delicious breakfast. For lunch try the grilled vegetable sandwich. Antique furniture and maroon walls add panache. Very lesbian friendly. $3-8.

Gravity Bar (415 Broadway E., 325-7186). A lezzie hot-spot on Capitol Hill, noted for its fabulous fruit and vegetable juice bar, as well as its vegetarian fare. Try the Hot Chapati roll-up, filled with melted provolone, parsley, tomato, green peppers and lemon tahini. $2-7.

Hana's Restaurant (219 Broadway E., 328-1187). A popular Capitol Hill sushi bar, and rightly so, which fills up quickly. Price depends on how much you eat. $3-whatever.

Julia's in Wallingford (4401 Wallingford Ave. N., 633-1175). Be prepared to stand in line for a wholesome, delicious, vegetarian weekend breakfast. Woman-owned. $5-10.

Mae's Phinney Ridge Cafe (65th and Phinney, 782-1222). Huge breakfast plates that start with homemade scones, coffee cake and cinnamon roles. Lesbian- and kid-friendly atmosphere, and near the Woodland Park Zoo. Open 7 a.m.-3 p.m. every day. $5-10.

The Easy (916 E. Pike, 323-8343). Remodeled recently with modern lighting and beautiful wood floors. Lunch and dinner are served daily — in the restaurant half of the building — and breakfast is served on weekends. The other half of the building is a women's dance hall. Lesbian-owned. $5-10.

Wildrose Tavern (1021 E. Pike, 324-9210). The best thing on the menu, is the "world famous" vegetarian cashew walnut burger, and anyone in the saloon setting will vouch for that. Happy hour is everyday from 4-7 p.m. Lesbian-owned. $4-10.

Coffeehouses

Where else in the world can you buy a cappuccino in an airport parking lot, or phone ahead to your favorite barista and have a cup waiting for you when you arrive?

Bauhaus Books and Coffee (301 Pine St., 625-1600). Housed in a large bookstore, in which the main activities are reading and sipping. Most people wear black.

Cafe Paradiso (1005 Pike St., 322-6960). The chairs are as creaky as the floors, but the coffee is dependably fresh, and the clientele is dependably on the gay side.

Dilettante (416 Broadway E., 329-6463). This cozy, candle-lit coffee and gourmet chocolate shop is always busy.

Espresso Roma (202 Broadway E., 324-1866). Quiet with simple decor and many regulars.

Rosebud Espresso and Bistro (719 E. Pike St., 323-6636). Comfy couches and cheery decor make this a tempting place to hide out from rainy weather. Very lesbian friendly. $2-7.

♪ PLAY-MEET

Bars

Timberline (2015 Boren, 622-6220). A mixed gay and lesbian country-western dance club.

The Easy (916 E. Pike, 323-8343). This huge women's dance club is located on Capitol Hill's main promenade. Darts, pool tables, dancing, DJs, as well as a formidable beer selection.

Wildrose Tavern (1021 E. Pike, 324-9210). In addition to serving great burgers, this is a good place to kick up your heels and dance with the locals.

Piano Bar

Kid Mohair (1207 Pine St., 625-4444). Classy gay dance bar with mood lighting on the outside, and illuminated stars on the ceiling inside. Wednesday is women's night. Hydrate yourself before entering; a glass of water costs 50 cents.

SHOP

General Shopping

Broadway Market (401 Broadway E., 323-4062). This lively Capitol Hill mall houses an array of national and local stores, intimate boutiques, restaurants and cafes — all of which are very gay popular. In fact, some of the best babe-watching in town is from the Gravity Bar juice bar on ground level.

Passport (123 Pine, 628-9799). Natural-fiber clothing from local, as well as international designers.

Pink Zone (211 Broadway E, 325-0050, or 800/762-LIPS). Tattoo and hair salon, accented with body piercing and "visibly queer gear."

Toys in Babeland (711 E. Pike St., 328-2914). Lesbian-owned "toy" and fantasy store located in Capitol Hill.

Westlake Center (Fifth Ave. and Pike St., 467-1600). The heart of downtown's retail marketplace, with **Nordstrom's** as its anchor — fondly known to locals as "Nordies." The monorail at Fifth Ave. and Pine St. transports travelers to Seattle Center and the Space Needle. Fare is 75 cents each way, and trains leave every 15 minutes.

Food Markets

Central Co-op (1835 12th Ave., 329-1545). A natural foods grocery store on Capitol Hill.

Pike Place Market (Pike St. and First Ave., 682-7453). Sixteen buildings of restaurants and shops, plus outdoor stalls filled with fresh

SEATTLE

seafood and produce, Northwest wines, and local arts and crafts. Plan a day of it.
Uwajimaya (519 Sixth Ave. S., 624-6248). Asian food and gift market, with produce, seafood, meats, a deli and souvenirs. Located two blocks east of the Kingdome under the blue tile roof.

Outdoor Gear

Many outdoor gear companies were born in Seattle, and several of these stores' bargain basements and posh retail outlets are scattered throughout the downtown area. There are **Eddie Bauer** (1330 Fifth Ave., 622-2766), **Feathered Friends** (1516 11th Ave., 324-4166), **Patagonia** (2100 First Ave., 622-9700) and **North Face** (1023 First Ave., 622-4111), which are good, general clothing and mountaineering stores. **REI** (222 Yale Ave. N., 223-1944) is the ultimate superstore, with the tallest indoor rock pinnacle, and *any* item can be tested in the rain room, on the bike track, or in the canoeing lake. **Warshal's** (1000 First [*gone*] Ave., 624-7300) has a huge, inexpensive selection of sports equipment, as well as the all-important rain gear.

Bookstores

Bailey/Coy Books (414 Broadway E., 323-8842, www.speakeasy.org/baileycoy). This lesbian-owned bookstore is in the heart of Capitol Hill, and has an impressive selection of lesbian fiction, as well as other feminist and mainstream literature.
Beyond the Closet Bookstore (518 E. Pike, 322-4609). An exclusively gay and lesbian bookstore in Capitol Hill.
Elliott Bay Bookstore (in Pioneer Square, 101 S. Main St., 624-6600). Stacks and stacks of every book imaginable.
Red & Black Books (432 15th Ave. E., 322-READ). Capitol Hill's oldest independent, cooperative bookstore.

123

🦋 KIDS' STUFF

Seattle Aquarium (Waterfront Park, Pier 59, 386-4320). An up-close look at Puget Sound's inhabitants, including a giant octopus. Adults, $7.15; children, $4.70.

Seattle Center (Fifth Ave. N. and Mercer St., 443-2111). The 74-acre entertainment complex houses the **Children's Museum** (441-1768), **Pacific Science Center** (443-2001), and the **Space Needle** (443-2100), for a panoramic view of Seattle.

Woodland Park Zoo (5500 Phinney Ave. N., 684-4600). Rated among the world's 10 best, the zoo features an African Savannah, a tropical rain forest and an Asian elephant forest. Adults, $7.50; children, $2.75.

☼ SPIRITUAL

Congregation Tikvah Chadashah (at the Prospect Congregation Church, 20th Ave. E. and East Prospect Ave., 329-2590). Puget Sound's gay and lesbian Jewish congregation.

Dignity Seattle (325-7314). Catholic mass for lesbians at St. Joseph's, 18th and Aloha Street, Sunday evenings at 7:30 p.m.

Gay Buddhist Fellowship (726-0051). Meets Fridays, 7 p.m.

Gays for Jesus (938-GAYS). Television program on channel 29, Wednesdays, 10:30 p.m.

Jewish Lesbians (322-3953). Meets the third Fridays of each month for potluck dinner and discussion.

MCC-Seattle (2101 14th Ave. S., 325-2421). Worship service Sunday at 11 a.m.; evening service at 6 p.m.

Plymouth Congregational Church (Sixth and University, 622-4865). Chapel, 9 a.m.; Forum, 10 a.m.; Sanctuary, 11 a.m.

Primitive Fire (781-2947). Spirit group meeting every other Wednesday at 7 p.m.

Spirituality Group (932-5615). A group for women who are either blocked on their current spiritual path, or just want to find one.

SEATTLE

RESOURCES

General Information

Seattle Visitor's Bureau (Washington St. Convention Center, 461-5840).

ALPS (233-8145). The Associated Lesbians of Puget Sound puts out a monthly newsletter announcing social and special-interest events.

Lesbian Cancer Support Group (522-0199).

Lesbian Resource Center (1808 Bellevue Ave., #204, 322-DYKE). One of the oldest community resource centers in the country turned 25 years old in 1996. The drop-in center is open Monday-Friday, 2-7 p.m.; Saturday, 12-5 p.m.

Seattle Bisexual Women's Network (783-7987).

Single Lipstick Lesbians (933-1190 or 313-5217). Dinner club for single femmes.

Women's AIDS/HIV Support Group (322-2159).

Media

Dyke TV. Fridays, 9:30 a.m., on cable channel 29.

LRC News (322-3965). Monthly newspaper published by the Lesbian Resource Center, and available at most bookstores for $1.

Seattle Gay News (324-4297, electra.cortland.com/sgn). Weekly gay and lesbian newspaper. 25 cents.

Seattle Weekly (623-0500). Seattle's alternative press, with event listings and schedules.

UltraViolet (322-3965). A quarterly magazine published by the Lesbian Resource Center.

Womanotes. An eclectic collection of women's music every Thursday night, 8-10 p.m., on 91.3 FM-KBCS.

Washington, D.C.

area code 202

WHAT TO EXPECT

Some people believe that once you have visited Washington, D.C., odds and ends in your life will suddenly come together. Bits of American history — as well as lesbian-American history — that have harbored in your brain since junior high will, finally, make sense. Needless to say, when you stand on the Capitol Building's steps facing the Washington Monument, and imagine an upcoming Names Project display on the lawn in between, the Lesbian Avenger in you — or maybe the lobbyist in you — will want to protest something. Doesn't everybody come to the nation's capital at least once in their lives to do that? All of the controversy surrounding same-sex marriage and Colorado's Amendment 2; the memory of the 1993 gay and lesbian March on Washington, whether you attended it or not; the AIDS walk festivals that will happen on the White House Ellipse; and the minuscule and somber Vietnam Women's Memorial ... your connections with all of those things that had previously been tangled up in your mind will come clearly to the forefront. Don't be surprised when you feel enraged and smart and opinionated and totally alive, all at once.

That's how people are in D.C. Ten out of every 10 people in the nation's capital have distinct opinions, one political party affiliation, and a few good protests under their belts. Within two hours of your arrival, you will probably be asked if you are a Democrat or Republican, how you felt when Nancy Reagan lit the White House Christmas tree by flipping a switch from her home in California, and if you would like to have your picture taken standing next to a life-sized cardboard statue of Hillary Clinton. And throughout your stay, people will be loading you up with similar political chotsky.

But despite Washington's diverse collection of people and opinions, the government — which is what Washington is all about, as it is one of the last single-industry cities in the U.S. — acts as a giant integrator. The gay and lesbian community is *not* ghettoized, though DuPont Circle is where most gay and lesbian businesses flourish. There, every other restaurant is gay-owned. But restaurants are frequented based on political affiliation, not sexuality — a protocol that was established 200 years ago.

Washington should be on every lesbian's list of destinations, as well as every lesbian's children's list, not just because of the political issues that are swatted back and forth from the House to the Senate like a badminton game. But it is, above all, a beautiful city. There are several hundred monuments and museums, most of which offer free admission. There are also fun neighborhoods such as gay DuPont Circle, a Bohemian Adams-Morgan and collegiate Georgetown that are historic, well-groomed and not federally governed.

And, finally, there is art. It is entirely possible to wander aimlessly through parks and plow into an amazing, yet little known sculpture nestled behind a wall of bougainvillea. Small community theaters pop up every autumn. In summer, the Washington Symphony conducts free concerts on the lawn in front of the Capitol Building. And there is usually an outdoor public art exhibit along Constitution Avenue.

Whichever course you choose — politicking or sightseeing — take note of the 19-foot bronze statue of the Native American woman atop the Capitol Building. When she was taken down to be cleaned a few years ago, even Washington's most powerful men were taken aback by her size and enormous metaphoric power. After all, the sun rises on her before it shines on the rest of the city.

What To Bring

The all-important blazer that can be worn with jeans or a skirt is essential. Also, bring an umbrella and walking shoes.

WASHINGTON, D.C.

Best Time To Visit

Mild temperatures from late March to May make dogwood and cherry trees blossom like mad.

Getting Around

Washington is one of the few capital cities in which a rental car is not necessary. Instead, ride the **Metrorail** or the **Metrobus** (637-7000 for both), and taxis are also plentiful. **Tour Mobiles** (703/979-0690) shuttle tourists to monuments and most other major attractions. A one-day ticket is $12, and if it's bought after 2 p.m., it's good for the rest of that day as well as all of the next day. The **Washington Flyer** (703/685-1400) bus or taxi will get you to and from the airports. Also, check out the **Washington Water Bus** (540/347-5111), which makes regular stops at the Lincoln and Jefferson Memorials, and other points along the Potomac River, then continues to Georgetown and Roosevelt Island. But the best way to experience city life is on foot.

STAY

Luxury

Hay-Adams Hotel (800 16th St. NW, 638-6600 or 800/424-5054). After opening in 1927, the hotel became Amelia Earhart's favorite place to stay while visiting Washington. It is large — 143 rooms — yet it is truly elegant. $145-270.

Guest Houses

Kalorama Guest House (2700 Cathedral Ave. NW, 328-0860). Two Victorian houses side-by-side near the Adams-Morgan neighborhood beckon the frugal traveler. Price includes laundry facilities, a continental breakfast, afternoon sherry, and fresh flowers in every room. It's close to the National Zoo, Metro and the Washington Cathedral. Very lesbian friendly. $55-95.

Tabard Inn B&B (1739 "N" St. NW, 785-1277). Located south of

DuPont Circle, with the atmosphere of a country inn, it's within walking distance of all the important things: Lammas women's bookstore and the Pop Stop. The attached restaurant uses produce from its own garden. Very lesbian friendly. $70-120.

SEE-DO

In and Around D.C.

Adams-Morgan Neighborhood (Columbia Rd. NW between 18th and Kalorama Park NW). An eclectic, international area with an array of restaurants, hip specialty stores and late-night entertainment.

Black History National Recreation Trail (619-7222). The trail leads people to sites in historic neighborhoods that illustrate aspects of African-American history. For a brochure, write to: 1100 Ohio Cr. SW, Washington, DC 20242.

Congressional Cemetery (18th and Potomac Streets SE). Skip the well-known Arlington Cemetery and check out this enchanting, unkempt one. In addition to paying respects to Belva Lockwood (the first woman to practice law before the Supreme Court), Anne Royall (a 19th Century adventurer and writer), and Adelaide Johnson (one of the original suffragettes), there are several memorials for gay men, as well. J. Edgar Hoover is buried two sites down from his longtime lover, Clyde Tolson. And Leonard Matlovich — the man who was given a dishonorable discharge from the Navy for being gay in 1975, and who died of AIDS in 1988 — carries his now-famous epitaph on his tombstone: "When I was in the military they gave me a medal for killing two men and a discharge for loving one."

Holocaust Memorial Museum (100 Raoul Wallenberg Pl. SW, 488-0400). A visit to this somber Memorial requires calling ahead for tickets (432-7328 or 800/551-7328) because the 2000 that are allotted per day usually sell out before noon. The permanent exhibition is not recommended for children under age 11.

National Arboretum (3501 New York Ave. NE, 544-8733). When the Capitol Building was refurbished in the late 1950s, its Corinthian

WASHINGTON, D.C.

columns were taken down and stashed east of the city. Years later, they were erected on a plot in the Arboretum, giving the gardens a look reminiscent of ancient Greek ruins.

National Museum of Women in the Arts (1250 New York Ave. NW, 783-5000). A permanent collection with more than 1500 works from at least 400 women, including painters Cassatt, Frida Kahlo and Georgia O'Keefe.

Rock Creek Park (426-6832). Urban sprawl meets the wilderness here in this enormous, inner city park. Mountain bike trails, picnic areas, playgrounds, tennis courts and the Horse Center make up only part of what the park has to offer.

Smithsonian Institution (1000 Jefferson Dr. SW, 357-2700). Nine of the Institute's 14 museums are located on the National Mall between the Washington Monument and the Capitol Building, including the popular **National Air and Space Museum** (Independence Ave. at Sixth St. SW, 357-1400), which displays Amelia Earhart's Lockheed Vega — the jalopy that sent the pilot soaring into history with her 1932 crossing of the Atlantic Ocean. At the **National Museum of American History** (14th St. and Constitution Ave. NW) you can see Mary Pickersgill's original 1813 Star Spangled Banner. After the flag survived the 1814 British attack on Washington, during the War of 1812, Francis Scott Key wrote what was to become the national anthem. Also, check out the original ruby slippers worn by Judy Garland in "The Wizard of Oz," and other American kitsch, such as Archie Bunker's chair.

Near D.C.

Takoma Park, Maryland (Bound by Piney Branch Rd., 14th Ave., Carroll Ave. and Georgia Ave.). This is a more settled, yet hip, lesbian and gay neighborhood, not far from downtown Washington, D.C. There is not much here for the traveler, but at least stop in the lesbian-owned **Savory Café** (7071 Carroll Ave., 301/270-2233), and the lesbian-frequented **Takoma Park Silver Spring Co-op** (623 Sligo Ave., Silver Spring, MD, 301/588-6093).

Chesapeake & Ohio Canal National Historic Park (301/739-

4200). This slim park stretches 184 miles from Georgetown to Cumberland, Maryland. The towpath is open to bikers, runners and hikers. Main entrance is at Great Falls, Maryland.

Mount Vernon Trail (703/285-2598). A 19-mile trail winds along the Virginia side of the Potomac River between Roosevelt Island and Mount Vernon; great for an afternoon bike ride.

KEEP FIT-RECREATION

Adventuring (703/521-0290). The local chapter of the International Gay and Lesbian Outdoor Organization, which partakes in just about any outing imaginable, except competitive sports and museum tours. Call for upcoming events.

D.C. Frontrunners (828-3223). Gay and lesbian runners, joggers and walkers meet every Saturday and Sunday morning at 23rd and "P" Streets in Rock Creek Park, 9 a.m.

Lambda Divers (265-3089). Lesbian scuba diving group.

Team D.C. Velo (703/204-0934). Gay and lesbian cyclists.

Wander Women (301/942-3176). Lesbian hiking and social group.

EAT

Fine Dining

Cities (2424 18th St. NW, 328-7194). Each year, the management unveils a new menu and decor that compliments whatever international city will be featured for the following 12 months. Florence, Istanbul, Hollywood and Hong Kong have been featured in recent years. Live music and dancing. In the Adams-Morgan neighborhood. $20-35.

Nora's (2132 Florida Ave. NW, 462-5143). What used to be a pleasant vegetarian restaurant *sans* the granola feel, has evolved into an upscale dining experience, with entrees such as potato-crusted halibut and veal in an anise-ginger sauce. Lesbian friendly. $18-30.

Trumpets (1603 17th St. NW, 232-4141). The cuisine is fussier than Californian, yet lighter than Continental — cumin grilled chicken breast, barbecued quail, grilled scallops. To get into the restaurant, meander through the often-packed bar (Wednesdays is women's night). Gay-owned. $10-25.

Casual Dining

Cafe Luna (1633 "P" St. NW, 387-7400). This good ole' carbo-enriched, basic Italian food joint is a frequent hangout for women in the DuPont Circle area. Gay-owned. $7-25.

Cafe Berlin (322 Massachusetts Ave. NE, 543-7656). Excellent homemade pastries, as well as German and American food. Lesbian owned. $7-15.

Mr. Henry's (601 Pennsylvania Ave. SE, 546-8412). Lesbians have been returning to this Capitol Hill pub for years, not only for the dependable, juicy burgers and Reubens, but for the lesbian clientele, as well. Live folk music Thursday-Saturday nights. $5-12.

Music City Roadhouse (1050 30th St. NW, 337-4444). The ultimate southern dive features a live gospel brunch every Sunday, and southern home cooking that's as good as grandma's. Start with the rich skillet corn bread, and don't stop until you've finished the boiled custard dessert. $10-25.

Coffeehouses

Coffeehouse for Women with HIV/AIDS (Brooks Mansion, 901 Newton St. NE, 301/459-1707). Meet, share and talk on Saturday evenings, 3-6 p.m. Children welcome.

Pop Stop (1513 17th St. NW, 328-0880). This popular lesbian hangout in DuPont Circle offers a plethora of lounging options, from the outdoor patio to the smokers' den to the couch potato chamber. As always, there is good company and conversation to be had.

Soho Tea and Coffee (2150 "P" St. NW, 463-7646).

GAY USA   Lori Hobkirk

🎵 PLAY-MEET

The Circle (1629 Connecticut Ave., 462-5575). The men's bar recently converted one of it's rooms into the Lipstick Lounge, which is open to women seven nights a week, and is staffed by women. It's laid back and quiet. No cover.

Hung Jury (1819 "H" St. NW, 785-8181). D.C.'s only exclusive women's bar is located in residential Foggy Bottom, and appeals mostly to the younger, intellectual crowd. Open Friday and Saturday nights only, except for special occasions such as Pride Fest.

Phase One (525 Eighth St. SE, in Capitol Hill, 544-6831). A southeast neighborhood bar, it's a fun, rowdy scene on weekends. Mostly women.

Trumpets (1603 17th St. NW, 232-4141). Wednesday nights is lesbian night in the bar.

💲 SHOP

General Shopping

Pavilion at the Old Post Office (1100 Pennsylvania Ave. NW, 289-2224). The former post office houses more than 80 one-of-a-kind shops and restaurants. Also, check out the dramatic view of downtown from the top of the original 315-foot clock tower.

Union Station (40 Massachusetts Ave. NE, 289-1908). A Beaux-Arts working train station that has been restored to house an indoor shopping area, as well. It's a good place to hide on rainy days.

Food Markets

Eastern Market (Seventh St. SE and North Carolina Ave., 544-5646). A year-round indoor food market, similar to the Pike Street Market in Seattle, though smaller. Occasionally, vendors spill out to the sidewalk and across the street to the basketball court.

Fresh Fields (4530 40th St. NW, 237-5800). The area's local

WASHINGTON, D.C.

gourmet health-food supermarket.

Pride Shopping

Outlook (1706 Connecticut Ave. NW, 745-1469). One-stop-shopping for lesbian gifts, cards, jewelry and accessories.

Bookstores

Lambda Rising (1625 Connecticut Ave. NW, 462-6969). The quintessential gay community bookstore stocks just about every gay and lesbian book in print — and even those that are out of print. There is also a great selection of videos, music, jewelry, gifts, greeting cards and periodicals.

Lammas Women's Books & More (1607 17th St. NW, 775-8218 or 800/955-2662). A clearinghouse for DC's women's community, complete with books, jewelry, clothing and information on local events. Check out the store's bulletin board, as well as its new digs.

Sisterspace and Books (1354 "U" St. NW, 332-3433). African-American women's bookstore.

KIDS' STUFF

Capital Children's Museum (800 Third St. NE, 543-8600). A unique educational complex that encourages children to touch, smell, taste and wear the exhibits.

DC Ducks (686-5464). These boats on wheels — which are rebuilt World War II amphibious vessels — tour the downtown area by land, then splash into the Potomac River.

National Geographic Society (1600 "M" St. NW, 857-7588). For children and adults alike, an interactive exhibit dedicated to teaching about the earth and its geography.

National Zoological Park (3000 block of Connecticut Ave. NW, 673-4800). One of the nation's oldest zoos, it is known for its collection of pandas and Bengal tigers.

☼ SPIRITUAL

Bet Mishpachah (833-1638). The gay and lesbian synagogue of the city.
Gay and Lesbian Catholics (1820 Connecticut Ave. NW, at St. Margaret's Episcopal Church in DuPont Circle, 387-4516).
Jewish Feminist Spirituality Group (828-3071). Meets Sundays, 4 p.m.
Presbyterians for Lesbian and Gay Concerns (703/379-2238). Meets at Westminster Church, 400 "I" Street, each month on the fourth Tuesday, at 7:30 p.m.
Women's Alliance for Theology, Ethics and Ritual (301/589-3150).

☎ RESOURCES

General Information

Washington, D.C. is the national headquarters for several lesbian activist groups, such as the **National Lesbian Political Action Committee** (467-6408), the **National Organization of Women** (1000 14th St. NW, 331-0066), and the **Lesbian Avengers** (301/779-1740).

Washington, D.C. Convention and Visitors Association (1212 New York Ave. NW, Suite 200, 347-2873).

Black Lesbian Support Group (at the Whitman-Walker Clinic, 1734 14th St. NW, 797-3593). Meets every second Saturday of the month, 3-5 p.m.

Bon Vivant (1407 "S" St. NW, 301/907-7920). D.C.'s premier lesbian social club. There is a weekly Friday wind down at **Larry's Lounge** (18th and "T" Streets NW), 5:30-8:30 p.m.

Gay-Lesbian Hotline (833-3234).

Lesbian Health Clinic (797-3565). By appointment only.

Lesbian Switchboard (628-4666). Nightly information and peer counseling.

Wonderful Older Women (703/335-2540). A monthly rap group for women over 35.

WASHINGTON, D.C.

Media

Dyke TV. Wednesdays, 9 p.m., Channel 25.

Lambda Book Report (462-7924, AOL keyword: Lambda). Monthly magazine that reviews every new gay and lesbian book published, plus author interviews.

Metro Arts Entertainment Weekly (588-5220). Humor, interviews, and local gay and lesbian news.

off our backs (234-8072). The nation's most serious feminist newspaper.

Washington Blade (797-7000, www.washblade.com). A fat, weekly gay and lesbian paper with news, reviews, features and calendar of events.

Woman's Monthly (703/527-4881). DC's premier women's newspaper, primarily focusing on upcoming lesbian events.

PART 2

Smaller Towns *and* Resorts

Boulder, Colorado

area code 303

WHAT TO EXPECT

As popular as Boulder is, it's a wonder more people don't call it home. Situated 30 miles northwest of Denver, the university town claims only 95,000 inhabitants, and often serves as a pit stop on the way to Rocky Mountain National Park. At least, that's how it was 20 years ago, before the downtown Pearl Street pedestrian mall was built. Since then, people have stuck around a little longer, if not to shop and get a bite to eat, then to catch some street entertainment. But really, anyone who has been in town more than a few years is considered an old-timer.

Take the lesbian community, for example, which is as transient as the town itself. There are always new faces at the bar, or women who lived in town years ago and recently returned. But even though there will always be the dykes who are either new to town or new to the scene, there are also the tight-knit old-timers who organized the community way, way back 15 to 20 years ago, which is dinosaur years in terms of Boulder. That was when "The Lesbian Connection," Boulder's lesbian social club, was formed. Of course, many of those foremothers have moved away, but some are still around. As a visitor, though, they can be difficult to find.

If Boulder's lesbian community seems hard to access, that's because other than softball games at the Mapleton Street ballfields, University of Colorado women's basketball games, the lesbian-owned Walnut Cafe, and the Yard of Ale, which is the only gay and lesbian bar in town, there aren't any regular hangouts to speak of. Even TLC has changed its monthly potluck format to more informal sporadic meetings, and always declares a hiatus during the summer.

One thing you can count on, though, is that to be where the women are, all you need to do is check out a gym, rock-climbing wall, pool, hiking trail or bike path. Boulder lesbians love to be outdoors. Because of Boulder's temperate climate and variety of terrain — from flatlands to the Rocky Mountains — the area has become the preferred training ground for many world-class health nuts. There are hundreds of wannabe Olympic cycling champions and wannabe Boston marathoners, as well as the *real* winners of those events, training on county roads and trails at any given moment. Needless to say, Boulderites are F-I-T.

For many people living in Boulder Valley, there couldn't be a more ideal place to live. The sun shines an average of 300 days per year, and city council spends more money acquiring open space land than it does on its police department. Its close proximity to Rocky Mountain National Park and the ski slopes is ideal. Not to mention the laid-back attitude that placed Boulder at the top of the "cool" map years ago. This is where people wear gym clothes to work, and where corporations have written "dog policies," allowing a maximum of six or seven pets in the office at one time. Some people think the casual attitude has gone too far, but it is what makes the place so endearing. Where else would parents feed their six-month-old Celestial Seasoning's iced Red Zinger tea? And where else would you be able to enroll in a "Dancing with Slinkies" class?

The biggest dilemma for a Boulder tourist, however, is not necessarily worrying about how to pack gear for five different sports, or how to adjust your attitude once you get here. It is the dilemma that everybody who visits Boulder has to face, sometimes for the rest of their lives, and that is the curse that was put on the town by Arapahoe Indian Chief Niwot before he died in 1864. Niwot found Boulder so pleasing that he declared that anyone who visited the area at least once would someday return. So, keep that in mind while packing your bags.

What To Bring

Dress for the outdoors, typically in baggy shorts, a T-shirt, a pile vest, and Tevas, Birkenstocks or hiking boots. In the summer, bring a raincoat and take it with you everywhere. It may be clear and dry until 3 p.m., but then, all hell breaks lose.

Best Time To Visit

In September, many of the summer tourists and afternoon rain showers have dissipated, and there is a lovely, cool crispness in the air.

Getting Around

From Denver International Airport, take the **RTD** bus (299-6000) to Boulder; $8 one way. Or the **Airporter** shuttle (444-0808) will drop passengers at major Boulder hotels for $14 ($26 round trip). If you rent a car, take Peña Boulevard south to I-70, west to I-270, then northwest on Highway 36 to Boulder.

Once in Boulder, there is no need for a rental car unless you yearn to flee town and head for the hills, which, of course, you probably will. In town, the **Hop** (447-8282) connects the Pearl Street Mall, University Hill, the University of Colorado and Crossroads Mall, and costs 75 cents; and the **Skip** (447-8282) is the north-south shuttle down Broadway. Any guesses what the next addition to the city's rapid transit may be? Rent mountain bikes or tandems at the woman-owned **Bikesmith** (Arapahoe Village Shopping Center, 443-1132). Otherwise, just walk — it's gorgeous.

STAY

Hotels

Hotel Boulderado (2115 13th St., 442-4344). One block from the Pearl Street Mall, this charming landmark houses four restaurants and nearly takes up a city block. Ask for one of the original rooms, rather than staying in the newer wing. $141-220.

Foot of the Mountain Motel (200 Arapahoe, 442-5688). Log cabins furnished with refrigerators are situated across the street from a park and playground. Children and pets allowed. $55-70.

Guest Houses

Boulder Victoria Historic Inn (1305 Pine St., 938-1300). Location, location. This charming, meticulously renovated home is two blocks from the Pearl Street Mall, and another short walk to foothills hiking trails. $95-175 includes breakfast, afternoon tea with scones and shortbread, and evening port wine. Lesbian friendly.

SEE-DO

In and Around Boulder

Boulder Museum of Contemporary Art (1750 13th St., 447-1633). Features work primarily by local visual and performing artists.

Chautauqua Park (Ninth and Baseline Rd., 442-3282). The small, active, and independent Chautauqua was formed in 1897 by a group of Texas schoolteachers who were seeking a serene environment in which to continue their summer studies. Now, the park has grown to 80 acres, and is surrounded by hiking trails that lead into Flatirons rock formations. Visit the ranger station in the park for trail maps. Some of the more favorite trails among the women's community are the **Enchanted Mesa Trail**, which runs the length of Boulder's north-south greenbelt at the base of the foothills; **Gregory Canyon Trail** is a moderate hike up part of Green Mountain; and the spectacular and challenging **Royal Arches Trail** will take you to the back of the Flatirons. If you drive up Flagstaff Mountain and park, you must obtain a $2 daily auto pass from the ranger station.

Colorado Music Festival (1525 Spruce St., 449-2413). Most summer concerts take place in the ancient, paper-thin-walled, crowded Chautauqua Park Auditorium, but you can beat the crowd by throwing a blanket on the grass surrounding the building and listening to the performance from underneath the stars.

E-Town (443-8696). A public radio show with a save-the-earth bent is taped before a live audience on Sunday nights at the Boulder Theater. $6.

BOULDER

National Center for Atmospheric Research (West up Table Mesa Drive, the road ends in a parking lot, 497-1174). Even though NCAR is a national weather center, and doesn't sound like a fun place to take a date, there are two art galleries on the premises, as well as a self-guided tour of the Mesa Lab, which includes viewing a tornado-style vortex and a chaotic pendulum. Take my word, they are worth the trip. And it's a good place to access several walking paths into the hills behind Boulder.

Pearl Street Mall (between 11th and 15th Streets). In Italy, an evening stroll is called a *passaggiata*. In Boulder, it's the "mall crawl." Friday and Saturday nights are the ideal times to take in its real charm, which actually spans Pearl Street from Eighth to 18th Streets, but the pedestrian-only section is only four blocks.

Walking Tours of Boulder (646 Pearl St., 444-5192). Tour historic neighborhoods, downtown or cemeteries, and learn the quirky secrets of this Bohemian place. Children under 10 are admitted free. $4.

Near Boulder

Celestial Seasonings (4600 Sleepytime Dr., in Gunbarrel, 581-1202). Touring the famous tea factory is similar to touring a brewery, but the high comes from mint-leaf fumes, not alcohol.

Eldorado Canyon State Park (494-3943). In Boulder's formative years — the 1920s and '30s — the town was known as a rehabilitation center for people with chronic lung diseases, particularly tuberculosis. A huge sanitarium was built on the west end of Mapleton Street, and residents were regularly taken to the healing waters of Eldorado Springs, seven miles south of town. Today, Eldorado Canyon is a rock-climber's haven, and water jugs can be filled from the fresh spring for 75 cents a pop.

Indian Peaks Wilderness Area (444-6600). The Continental Divide south of Longs Peak is a 45-minute drive from Boulder. Trail heads at the Brainard Lake parking lot will take you up paths that lead to pristine alpine lakes and meadows.

Rocky Mountain National Park (970/586-1206). One of the most spectacular and serene wilderness areas anywhere. It is most impressive at sunrise and sunset when all the critters — especially herds of elk and deer — come out to graze. Pick up maps at the Beaver Meadows Visitor's Center on the west end of Estes Park. A seven-day pass is $10. If you traverse Trail Ridge Road to the west side of the Park, spend a couple of nights at the lesbian-owned, custom built **Spirit Mountain Ranch** in Grand Lake (970/887-3551); $100 includes a hot breakfast, dips in the hot tub, and endless hikes on the women's land.

Keep Fit-Recreation

There are more than 30 miles of cycling and running paths in the city of Boulder, and more than 100 miles of hiking trails in the parks and open space system. On most of those paths dogs are welcome on a leash and mountain bikers abound. The Boulder Chamber of Commerce sells Mountain Parks trail maps for $4. Also, stop by the Chautauqua Park Ranger Station for more maps and information.

Women on Two Wheels (449-2453). Meets the second and fourth Saturdays of the month, from April to October, for road or mountain bike rides in Boulder County. The energetic leader welcomes all abilities.

Women's Outdoor Club (271-3576). A lesbian club with both a Denver and Boulder branch that organizes hikes, back-country ski trips, mountain biking, and an annual winter retreat in the mountains.

EAT

Fine Dining

Dandelion (1011 Walnut, 443-6700). Of all the greens dished up in this delicious restaurant, sadly, dandelions are not among them. Instead, seared bass with ginger sauce and tuna steak in red wine typically make the special's list. Also, try the innovative potato lasagne. $12-30.

Flagstaff House (on Flagstaff Rd., 442-4640). One-and-a-half miles up Flagstaff Mountain Road are spectacular views of Boulder Valley and an impeccable French-Continental cuisine. Indulge in chateaubriand, lobster, or more exotic dishes such as rattlesnake and

BOULDER

wild alligator. $25-50 for main course.

Casual Dining

Chautauqua Dining Hall (in Chautauqua Park at Ninth and Baseline, 440-3776). Open only from May to September, the old place has a New England flavor to it, with hardwood floors and quilts hanging on the walls. Weekend brunches are popular. Put your name on the list early, and be prepared to wait. $5-15.

Dot's Diner (799 Pearl St., 449-1323). The music is a bit raucous, and the wait staff is usually toasted from the night before. Sometimes they don't even show up. But the dive, located in half of an old gas station, has the best sizzling huevos rancheros in town. Breakfast and lunch only. $3-10.

Naropa Institute Cafe (2130 Arapahoe, 546-3530). Boulder's best-kept vegetarian secret. Every selection is magnificent, from the Mexican lasagne, to the hummus, to the tempeh and vegetables. Make it a picnic on the grassy area behind the school. Very lesbian friendly. Lunch only while school is in session. $2-6.

Rio Grande Mexican Restaurant (1101 Walnut, 444-3690). While the green chile and homemade tortillas are excellent, the margaritas are coveted — the limit is three. Go forth and slurp wisely. $3-12.

Sushi Zanmai (1221 Spruce St., 440-0733). Sit at the sushi bar and make friends with the people who are making your meal, or grab a hibachi table in the dining room. Either way, the fish (for a land-locked city) is incredibly fresh and tasty, as if the ocean were out the back door. Happy hour is 4-7 p.m. $8-35.

Walnut Cafe (3073 Walnut, 447-2315). Lesbian Central. There is a constant turnover of women in the booths. The cafe stays open late after C.U. women's basketball games, and Tuesdays have been unofficially declared "pie night," which is a good excuse for socializing. Lesbian owned. $3-10.

Zolo Grill (2525 Arapahoe Rd., 449-0444). Creative Southwestern cuisine such as rellenos stuffed with goat cheese, and duck tacos. The burger is one of the best in town. For appetizers, try the fabulous guacamole. Lesbian friendly $7-15.

Coffeehouses

Trident Booksellers and Cafe (940 Pearl St., 443-3133). Vintage Boulder. The best place to eavesdrop. More of an old-timers hangout, and very lesbian friendly. $1-4.

Vic's (2680 Broadway, 440-8209). The speediest coffee service in town, as well as the choice spot for Boulder's young and affluent, including the lesbian crowd. Decor is 1950s combined with techno-fusion-chic. It's also a few storefronts from **Moe's Broadway Bagels** (2650 Broadway, 444-3252). The two go hand-in-hand.

PLAY-MEET

The Yard of Ale (2690 28th St., Unit C, 443-1987). The only gay and lesbian bar in town. Since Boulder's non-smoking ordinance passed in 1995, the bar has split into two sections — the front half is the smokers' lounge, and the back is for dancers and nonsmokers. Enter the dance floor via the safe alley to avoid the smoke. Woman-owned.

SHOP

General Shopping

Many unique shops and galleries are squeezed between several larger chain stores along the pedestrian-only **Pearl Street Mall** (between 11th and 15th Streets). Check out the **Boulder Arts and Crafts Coop** (1421 Pearl, 443-3683), **Jila's** designer dress shop (2035 Broadway, 442-0130), **Peppercorn** gourmet kitchen shop (1235 Pearl, 449-5847), and **Into the Wind** kite store (1408 Pearl, 449-5906). **Aria** (2043 Broadway, 442-5694) is a gay-owned, imaginative collection of home furnishings, lotions, refrigerator magnets and rainbow paraphernalia that is one-half block north of the Mall.

Elsewhere in town, check out **McGuckin Hardware** (2525

BOULDER

Arapahoe, 443-1822). Parts are parts, but anybody who is a tinkerer at heart will appreciate this everything-under-the-sun conglomeration of dealy-bobs.

Food Markets

Boulder County Farmers' Market (13th Street between Canyon and Arapahoe, 494-4997). Every Saturday morning and Wednesday afternoon, from late spring through early fall, organic farmers, flower vendors, food peddlers and musicians gather in downtown Boulder ... and *you* should be there too.

Wild Oats (2584 Baseline Rd., 499-7636; and its vegetarian market at 1825 Pearl St., 440-9599) and its sister store, **Alfalfa's** (1651 Broadway at Arapahoe, 442-0909), are both natural foods giants, and will have everything you need.

Bookstore

Word Is Out Women's Bookstore (1731 15th St., 449-1415). The store is filled with a wonderful selection of women's books, magazines, jewelry, CDs, cards and gifts. The owner is always knowledgeable about women's events happening around town.

🦋 KIDS' STUFF

Collage Children's Museum (2065 30th St., 440-9894). "Please touch" is the rule.

Fun-N-Stuff (4800 N. 28th St., 442-4FUN). Go-carts, batting cages and miniature golf — which, by the way, is an extremely challenging course.

☼ SPIRITUAL

Despite a community uproar a few years ago when a lesbian Presbyterian choir director was asked to resign, all of Boulder's churches and temples rang their bells simultaneously for one hour the day that antigay Amendment 2 was defeated by the U.S. Supreme Court — in support of diversity, of course.

Boulder Gay-Les-Bi Concerned Catholics (442-2864).

Karma Dzong Buddhist Temple (1345 Spruce, 444-0190). Meditation sittings are daily, 7:30-8:30 a.m., and Sunday mornings, 9-12 a.m.

Unity of Boulder (2855 Folsom, 442-1411).

RESOURCES

General Information

Boulder Chamber of Commerce (2440 Pearl St., 442-1044). Sells the "Boulder Bicycling and Pedestrian Map" for $2.50, and can answer any other sightseeing questions.

The Lesbian Connection (443-1105). Boulder's social lesbian organization. Call ahead to get a newsletter of upcoming potlucks and other events, such as the "Dykes with Dogs Hike" and the "Lesbians Invade Alfalfa's" evenings.

Media

Boulder Daily Camera (442-1202, www.bouldernews.com). The "Friday" section of the city's daily newspaper lists weekend events.

Circles (417-1385). Boulder's monthly lesbian news magazine.

This Way Out (449-4885). A gay- and lesbian-oriented radio news-magazine, Mondays, 6:30 p.m., on public radio KGNU 88.5-FM.

Weird Sisters (970/482-4393). The state's only all-lesbian monthly includes a column by local Lambda Literary Award winner Ellen Orleans.

BOULDER

DENVER (AREA CODE 303)

🥕 EAT

Casual Dining

Basil's (30 S. Broadway, 698-1413). Homemade Italian food. The four-pestos plate is an ideal choice. Very lesbian friendly. $7-18.

Racine's (850 Bannock St. at Speer, 595-0418). A large, hip, mainstream eatery with something for everybody, from burritos to tofu stir fries. Sunday brunch attracts the lesbian crowd. $4-14.

Denver Detour (551 E. Colfax, 861-1497). A lesbian-owned bar and Mexican food restaurant that caters to the Capitol Hill neighborhood. $3-10.

Coffeehouses

Common Grounds (3484 W. 32nd Ave., 458-5248). The coffeehouse of choice in lesbian-populated northwest Denver. Owned by a mother-daughter team, it's warm and comfortable. Live music is featured at least four nights a week.

Java Creek (287 Columbine St., 377-8902). A small and refreshing Cherry Creek coffee hang-out. Creative breakfasts and lunches are also available. Lesbian owned. $1-5.

🎵 PLAY-MEET

Ms. C's (7900 E. Colfax, 322-4436). A large, country-western women's bar 50 miles from Boulder. It's always packed, including the dance floor.

Sirens (2151 Lawrence, 297-0015). Every Friday night, this is Denver's lesbian hot spot, with be-bop, acid jazz and funk. No cover until 10 p.m.

The Elle (716 W. Colfax, 572-1710). A lesbian-only club featuring a series of rooms and moods, including the "lava" room, with a laid-back atmosphere with incense and lava lamps. Open Wednesday-Sunday.

SHOP

Pride shopping

Unique of Denver (2626 E. 12th Ave., 355-0689). Candles, stationery, magazines, jewelry and unusual gifts — all with a gay and lesbian theme.

Bookstore

The Book Garden (in Denver, 2625 E. 12th, 399-2004 or 800/279-2426). A sweet women's store with beautiful displays of gifts, jewelry and books. Call ahead for a newsletter.

RESOURCES

General Information

Gay and Lesbian Community Center of Colorado (831-6268). In Denver, it's the nearest community center to Boulder.

Media

Out Front (778-7900). Denver's gay and lesbian weekly. Heavy on the entertainment scene.

Quest (722-5965). Denver's monthly gay and lesbian newspaper with juicy, lengthy articles.

Westword (296-7744, www.westword.com). Denver-Metro area's hip entertainment weekly.

Northampton, Massachusetts

area code 413

WHAT TO EXPECT

While driving by Northampton on Interstate 91 in western Massachusetts, you think it might be just another New England town. Of course, the town probably grows some pretty good apples in the fall, as well as harvests tasty maple syrup in the spring, much like the nearby state of Vermont. But, from the highway, it is hard to know exactly what Northampton has to offer.

Well, get off the highway, girl! The truth is that Northampton is an old, picturesque mill town situated in the Connecticut River Valley. It has one traffic light, more bookstores than a small town deserves, and a severe shortage of restaurants. First impressions might have you thinking that Northampton women read more than they eat. Wait. Women? Did somebody say women? Park the car as soon as you can. Otherwise you might be accused of being a rubber-necking looky-loo — there are *so* many women.

That's right. Statistics suggest that one in three residents is a lesbian — ten thousand of thirty thousand people. It is hard to say how much of a role the all-woman Smith College has played in this explosive statistic over the years (which came first, the chicken or the egg?, but Northampton's reputation of being *the* spot where lesbians are settling to have kids and raise families is well-deserved. Residents, although biased, say it is the best town in America for lesbian nesting, due in part to its social and intellectual college atmosphere, as well as its liberal

Massachusetts political climate. Incredibly, the Northampton newspaper regularly prints commitment ceremonies and baby announcements. And one lesbian-owned Bed & Breakfast claims that more than 120 of its former guests have moved to the area (so be careful where you stay). There are so many women in this tiny town that the women's softball league regularly supports at least eighteen teams, and the banner for the Northampton gay-male contingent at the 1993 March on Washington read "Fags from Lesbianville."

And hundreds of Lesbianville dykes are soon-to-be-Lesbianville mothers. Evidence of that is the recent maternity ward expansion at the Northampton hospital. Be careful walking down Main Street; it has become a thoroughfare for baby carriages, with many lesbians at their helms.

Be aware, Northampton is not a party town by any means, so don't go looking for a wild and hapless time. It is a place to go to be visibly gay, live a happy life, procreate, and, of course, read. Women move to Northampton to be part of a nurturing community, a place where they can kiss and hold hands in public. Resident lesbians don't have to hide in Northampton, and, as a tourist, you won't either. Don't be surprised when you bump into a long, lost girlfriend who, you discover, has already moved to Northampton and asks, in all sincerity, when you will be moving there as well.

What To Bring

Northampton dykes tend to sport the "earth mother" look, perhaps even more than the women in Seattle and Boulder. Knee-length cotton skirts, T-shirts, tank tops and sandals fare well in this college town. Short, stylish hair is a must.

Best Time To Visit

The fall is especially nice, although quite touristy. If you plan to visit then, be sure to make reservations far in advance. And since the area is congested with colleges, you might want to avoid graduation and parents' weekends.

NORTHAMPTON

Getting There

The nearest major airport is Bradley International in Windsor Locks, Connecticut, 45 minutes south. Logan International Airport, in Boston, is two hours away. And Northampton has its own small airport with daily commuter service to New York and Boston, as well as Martha's Vineyard, Hyannis and Nantucket. If renting a car from Boston, take Interstate 90 — also known as "Mass Pike" — west to Interstate 91, then north to exits 18 or 19.

🗝 STAY

Luxury

Hotel Northampton (36 King St., 584-3100). An elegant, traditional New England inn with the graciousness of a grand hotel. Site of the annual Gayla Women's New Year's Eve celebration. $125-200.

Guest Houses

Apple Valley B&B (1180 Hawley Rd., Ashfield, 625-6758). Two Victorian rooms in a country hill town northwest of Northampton. Women only. $65.

Innamorata B&B (47 Main St., Goshen, 268-0300). Ten miles from Northampton. Weekday stays come without the breakfast. No children or pets. Women only. $70.

Ivy House B&B (1 Sunset Court, Amherst, 549-7554). Handsomely restored 1740s colonial (the bathrooms are inside, now) in the heart of Amherst. Two rooms: one has a queen bed, the other has two singles. Lesbian friendly. $60-80.

Little River Farm (968 Huntington Rd., Worthington, 238-4261). A working farm that's more like a petting zoo in the Berkshire Hills, thirty minutes from Northampton. There are donkeys, ducks, chickens, and forty acres of hiking space, extending into the Berkshires. Breakfast usually includes farm-fresh eggs. Open from early spring through late October. Women only. $75.

Old Red Schoolhouse and Lesbian Towers (584-1228). The schoolhouse was civil right's activist Sojourner Truth's house, and was originally built in the 1800s as a school. It has since been renovated into five upscale women's guest apartments. The Towers are in a small village three minutes from Northampton. Women only in the towers. $75-99.

Tin Roof B&B (586-8665). A turn-of-the-century farmhouse in the scenic Connecticut River Valley five minutes from Northampton, complete with a weight room. It was one of the original women's guest houses in the area, and now the owner has branched out into maintaining a Christmas tree farm, as well. $60.

SEE-DO

In and Around Northampton

Don Muller Gallery (40 Main St., 586-1119). A showplace of contemporary hand-blown glass, ceramics and jewelry — especially commitment rings.

Forbes Library (20 West St., 584-8399). Northampton prides itself on this gem, which locals consider the best library in the county, and is funded solely by an inheritance from a former Northampton judge. Within the library is the **Calvin Coolidge Memorial Room** with letters, papers, speeches, scrapbooks and memorabilia of the 30th President, who resided in Northampton for 38 years.

Historic Northampton (46 Bridge Rd., 584-6011). Historic Northampton maintains three houses dating back to the town's formative years that are definitely worth touring.

Lyman Plant House and Botanical Gardens (Smith College, 584-2700). Contained within these steamy rooms are plants from throughout the world in an 11,000 square foot greenhouse, including several herbaceous gardens. There is also a chrysanthemum show in the fall and a bulb show in the spring.

Smith College Museum of Art (Elm St. at Bedford Terrace, 585-2760). The museum's collection numbers approximately 24,000 objects, including a terrific representation of 19th and 20th Century European

NORTHAMPTON

and American art. Frequently, exhibits feature women's works.

The Sappho-nics (527-9581). Catch a concert of Northampton's own lesbian chorus. Call for concert times.

Near Northampton

Arcadia Nature Center and Wildlife Sanctuary (127 Coombs Rd., in Easthampton, 584-3009). A 550-acre site near the famed "great curve" of the Connecticut River Oxbow, which lies north of Mount Holyoke. It is a permanent sanctuary for birds and other forms of wildlife.

Chesterfield Gorge (left off Route 143, just past the Westfield River bridge). Gentle walking trails along a breathtaking chasm.

Dinosaur Footprint State Park (Route 5 south of Northampton). For five- to 50-year-olds, there are lots of easy walking trails, some leading to the remnants of ancient reptiles. The pull-out parking lot is on the east side of the road and is not marked. If you reach the traffic lights at Mountain Park, you have gone too far south.

Emily Dickinson House (280 Main St., Amherst, 542-8161). Selected rooms of the old homestead are open for guided tours from May through October. Most of the house is used as Amherst College English Department offices, but the poet's bedroom and writing desk are still intact.

Fall Foliage Tours The best known highway to view the changing colors in the Pioneer Valley is the Mohawk Trail, which is Route 2 from Orange to Williamstown. Other popular tours include Route 9 from Northampton to Pittsfield; Route 116 from Amherst to Ashfield; Route 63 in North Amherst north to Northfield; Route 202 from Belchertown north along the west side of the Quabbin Reservoir; Route 5 north from Whateley to Brattleboro, Vermont; west on Route 9 to Wilmington; south on Route 100 to Jacksonville; and southeast on 112 to Shelburne Falls. That pretty much covers the area.

Holyoke Heritage State Park (534-1723). The visitors's center features permanent exhibits on local history, industry, immigration, environment and self-guided sidewalk tours.

Volleyball Hall of Fame (444 Dwight St., Holyoke, 536-0926).

Since volleyball was invented in Holyoke in 1895, this is a fitting location for the extensive collection of memorabilia and displays that offer a chronology of the sport. There is also a computer panel that is programmed to answer any question you might have about the game.

KEEP FIT-RECREATION

Venture Out (584-3145). A gay and lesbian outing group that partakes in hiking, cycling and camping in the summer, and tours of museums and greenhouses in the winter.

EAT

Fine Dining

Green Street Cafe (64 Green St., 586-5650). Near Smith College theaters, Botanical Gardens and Fine Arts Museum. An intimate European-style cafe with a private garden, fireplace and great food. Gay-owned. $5-20.

Spoletos (50 Main St., 586-6313). A perennial favorite for creative Italian cuisine and incomparable atmosphere. It's one of the more noticeable restaurants along Main Street. $6-18.

Squires' Smoke and Game Club (132 Main St., on Route 9, Williamsburg, 268-7222). A quirky, elegant place along the river, and a hearty meal, make for an unforgettable evening (or maybe that's a quirky meal that makes for an elegant evening). Java Duck, Bangkok Game Hen and K.C. Blues Ribs are some of the entrees. $14-20.

Casual Dining

Bela's (68 Masonic St., 586-8011). Spicy vegetarian with great tofu and pastas. Lesbian-owned. $5-14.

Eastside Grill (19 Strong Ave., 586-3347). A little bit of everything: Delmonico steak, chicken etouffée, scallops Diane and grilled catfish. $5-15.

Fire & Water (5 Old South St., 586-8336). Vegetarian sandwich-

NORTHAMPTON

es, soups, salads and ice cream. Also, live poetry and music every night. $3-6.

La Cazuela (7 Old South St., 586-0400). The cuisines of Mexico and the American Southwest. Brunch is served Saturdays and Sundays. $8-11.

Paul & Elizabeth's (150 Main St., 584-4832). A natural foods restaurant serving pasta, seafood and rice dishes, and fresh baked bread. $5-9.

Sylvester's (111 Pleasant St., 586-5343). Count on a line outside the door for breakfast. There are three varieties of home fries and four kinds of pancakes. It's hearty and healthy for all of you carbo-queens. $4-8.

The India House (45 State St., 586-6344). Northampton's original Indian restaurant, serving the favorites mattar paneer and tandoori shrimp. $8-17.

Coffeehouses

Coffee Connection (211 Main St., 582-0041). Fresh, rich coffee for the connoisseur. Elegant desserts, as well. $2-6.

Haymarket Bookstore Cafe (Cracker Barrel Alley, 586-9969). A politically correct place that provides a free meeting space for groups working for social justice. Draws a younger set. $1-5.

La Fiorentina (19 Armory St., 586-7693). Homemade Italian pastries made from recipes dating back three generations. $2-5.

♪ PLAY-MEET

Our Hideaway (16 Bolduc Lane, Chicopee, 534-6426). A nice change from the bigger, louder clubs. Dancing Friday and Saturday nights, and never a cover charge. Mostly women.

Pearl Street Nightclub (10 Pearl St., 584-7771). A mixed straight, gay and lesbian bar, with live music most nights. Sunday is women's night.

The Grotto (25 West St., 586-6900). A small and intimate gay and lesbian bar, cafe and dance club. Quiet during the week, but packed on weekends.

$$$ SHOP

Food Markets

Atkins Farms Country Market (Corner of Bay Road and Route 116, south of Amherst, 253-9528). The market has a delightful middle-of-nowhere feel, but it's actually a few miles south of Amherst. A complete array of fresh produce, juices, as well as a delectable bakery.

Cornucopia Foods (10 Main St., 586-3800). A large selection of homeopathic remedies, herbs, vitamins, and the regular organic whole foods selection.

Pride Shopping

Pride and Joy (20 Crafts Ave., 585-0683). Lesbian, gay and bisexual gifts, cards, clothing and jewelry. Each day at 4 p.m. everybody in the store watches the "Rosie O'Donnell Show." It's become a regular social event.

Gifts

Annie's Garden and Gift Store (515 Sunderland Rd., Route 116, Amherst, 549-6359). An unusual assortment of pleasurable things: organic gardening supplies and Annie's pickles, jams, chutneys, vinegars and honeys. Lesbian-owned.

Wild Iris (7 Old South St., 586-7313). Gifts by women artists with women in mind.

Clothing

Cathy Cross for Women (151 Main St., 586-9398). Trendy, exciting clothes.

Country Comfort (153 Main St., 584-0042). Casual and contemporary natural fibers clothing, jewelry, scarves and socks.

NORTHAMPTON

Motherwear (586-3488). Where else but in Northampton would there be a catalog company specializing in clothes for nursing mothers, diapering supplies, natural baby products and parenting books?

Square One Presents (24 Pleasant St., 585-1118). Sophisticated clothing and a vast selection of designer watches.

Bookstores

Beyond Words Book Shop (189 Main St., 586-6304). Northampton's largest full-service book shop with music, gifts, stationery, and a bountiful children's selection.

Food for Thought Books (106 N. Pleasant St., Amherst, 253-5432). A nonprofit workers' collective carrying a wide selection of progressive books.

Third Wave Feminist Bookstore (90 King St., 586-7851). Lesbian-owned and operated shop that stocks new and rare selections. The store has become a lesbian institution in Western Massachusetts.

KIDS' STUFF

Look Memorial Park (300 N. Main St., 584-5457). This recreational park has tennis courts, a miniature train, pedal boats, a zoo, and an outdoor theater.

Words and Pictures Museum of Fine Sequential Art (140 Main St., 586-8545). An interactive comic art museum for both kids and adults.

SPIRITUAL

Grace Community Church (532-5060).
Hope Community Church (20 Gaylord St., Amherst, 253-2522).
Integrity (532-5060). Episcopalian gay and lesbian group.

RESOURCES

General Information

Northampton Chamber of Commerce (62 State St., 584-1900, www.noho.com).
Bi Women's Support Group (582-0452 or 582-0305).
De Colores (253-3470 or 584-7280). A social group for lesbians of color, with a potluck on the last Sunday of each month.
Everywoman's Center (Wilder Hall, U-Mass, 545-0883 or 545-2436 for hotline). A major resource center with information and referrals.
Kaleidoscope (773-3092 or 525-2188). A group for gays, lesbians and bisexuals older than 55.
L.E.A.H. (586-1125). Health care of lesbians.
Northampton Area Lesbian and Gay Business Guild (585-8839, www.westmas.com/nalgbg/).
U-Mass Lambda Line (545-2632). Complete listing of meetings, events and community resources.
Stonewall Center (U-Mass, Amherst, 545-4824, www.umass.edu/stonewall). A lesbian, bisexual, gay and transgender educational center.

Media

The Lesbian Calendar (586-5514). A great publication highlighting the area's events. $3 per month or $35 per year.
Women Unlimited Magazine (733-1231). Monthly women's guide to western Massachusetts.
Advocate (247-9301, www.newmassmedia.com). A news and arts weekly for the Pioneer Valley published out of Hatfield, Massachusetts. Not necessarily gay-oriented.
Optimist (586-7070). An arts weekly for the Pioneer Valley, published out of Northampton.

Palm Springs, California

area code 760

WHAT TO EXPECT

To lesbians, Palm Springs is synonymous with the prestigious Nabisco-Dinah Shore LPGA golf tournament that takes place here in late March. The two go hand in hand. You say the word "Dinah" and visions of 30,000 women taking over the desert southwest come to mind. You see a woman tee-ing off in Anywhere, USA, and you think of the sweltering heat of Palm Springs, the sleepy mornings that linger in the hills — okay, perhaps that is smog — and a sexual energy that is about as hot as metal golf clubs in 110-degree heat. Yikes!

Once in Palm Springs, however, it's not only Queen Dinah that rules, but memories of the 1950s and 60s American space race, as well. Much of the city's architecture looks like something out of a "Jetsons" scene. And the jewels and clothing in second-hand stores and 1960s "antique" shops are equally as futuristic. Fashion follows suit with big hair and pointy sunglasses being the rage. Cadillacs outnumber economy-size cars, and, it seems, lava-lamps were invented here. It's not a case of history repeating itself; it's a matter of time moving at the same pace it took the glaciers of the northern hemisphere to melt.

For women seeking a place to unwind and relax, the year-round, fair-weather resorts of Palm Springs ante up. The routine is to get up as late as possible, every day, and do nothing. That is, only do something if you really must, but spend the entire day thinking about what you think you might want to do. One possibility is to cruise down Dinah Shore Drive while popping locally grown dates into your mouth, window shop in nearby Cathedral City and Rancho Mirage, count the Dean Martin lookalikes on Palm Canyon Drive, and then cool off beneath the misting machines that surround every hotel and swimming pool. Also, consider taking the aerial tramway to the top of the San Jacinto mountains and hiking around at an elevation of nearly 9000-feet — a good 15-20 degrees cooler than the valley floor. And if you never get around to doing any of these well-thought-out activities, hey, it's okay. You are on the right track.

After all, Palm Springs *is* a resort town. It always has been, and probably always will be. Women who are "night" people will have it made in a town like this, but for "morning" people it will take some acclimatizing, possibly something akin to recovering from jet lag. For example, hotel poolside breakfasts aren't served until 10 a.m., and most coffee shops don't open until noon, including the gay-owned and operated Village Pride Coffee Shop. And noon on the west coast is 3 p.m. on the east coast. But you'll be so relaxed and busy tanning that caffeine will be the last thing on your mind. Trust me.

What To Bring

Anything that's cool and comfortable over a swimsuit. Once you get to a lesbian-only hotel, you won't have to wear anything up top. Early morning coffee addicts should pack a jar of instant coffee and a hot pot.

Best Time To Visit

In the fall, temperatures cool down, the wind stops blowing, tourists go home for a few months, and the lesbian scene remains active. Gay pride is in November, as well as the gay and lesbian tennis tournament, which is Thanksgiving weekend. Another primo time to visit, of course, is at the end of March for the Nabisco-Dinah Shore LPGA championship.

Getting There

From Los Angeles International Airport take Century Boulevard (Highway 105) east, Interstate 405 north, then I-10 east approximately 130 miles to the Highway 111 turn off to Palm Springs. Highway 111 becomes Palm Canyon Drive, which is the main drag through town. Or

PALM SPRINGS

from LAX, hop on a connecting flight to the Palm Springs airport.

Getting Around

Rent a car at either at the Los Angeles or the Palm Springs airport. Or you can rely on the gay-owned **Rainbow Cab Company** (327-5702 or 320-2964).

STAY

Luxury

Korakia Pensione (257 S. Patencio Rd., 864-6411). A whitewashed vision of Greece. Many writers and artists from Los Angeles stay here because the conversation is witty, the furniture is hand-crafted, and the feather beds are pure fluff. $100-170.

Hotels

Bee Charmer Inn (1600 E. Palm Canyon Dr., 778-5883). A small, yet charming 13-roomed bungalow. Each room has a microwave and refrigerator. Women only. No children or pets. Reservations recommended. $77-97.

Desert Palms Inn (67-580 Hwy. 111, Cathedral City, 324-3000 or 800/801-8696). A hub of many parties during LPGA time, the 29-room retreat is ideal for socialites because of its large courtyard with a giant pool and Jacuzzi. Gay men and women are both welcome. $49-109.

The Enclave (641 San Lorenzo Rd., 325-5269). Continental breakfast is served poolside, and there is a fairly thorough lesbian video library to peruse. The pink bathroom towels are a nice touch. Very lesbian friendly. $60-125.

Economy

Motel 6 (595 E. Palm Canyon Dr., 325-6129). A very nice, clean motel for the money. Centrally located. $33-50.

GAY USA   Lori Hobkirk

SEE-DO

In and Around Palm Springs

Aerial Tramway (Take Tramway Road off Highway 111, 3.5 miles up the hill, 325-4227). A "must do" while in the valley. The 80-passenger, Swiss-built tram climbs 8516 feet up San Jacinto Mountain, where it's much cooler than the desert floor. At the top, the 13,000-acre Mt. San Jacinto Wilderness State Park is a great place to hike. Adults, $16; children, $11.

Celebration Playhouse (210 E. Arenas, 416-9299). An exclusively gay- and lesbian-oriented theater. Its season runs October-March.

Coachella Valley Preserve (343-1234). The last undisturbed watershed in the region. Hiking trails — desert and mountain — reveal fringe-toed lizards, roadrunners and quails in a weirdly beautiful landscape.

Magic Carpet Rides (68-688 Perez Rd., Cathedral City, 321-8170). Admit it. You have always wanted to put a Harley Davidson between your legs. Anyone with a motorcycle license can rent one of these two-wheeled pleasure troves, from the basic Sportster to the legendary Fat Boy. $100-150 for five hours; $150-200 for 24 hours.

Moorten Botanical Garden (1701 S. Palm Canyon Dr., 327-6555.) A living museum, with nature trails, and thousands of varieties of giant cacti, trees, birds and flowers. There is usually a good art exhibit, as well.

Palm Springs Desert Museum (101 Museum Dr., 325-7186). The museum has a triple focus on fine art, natural science and the performing arts. It also offers nature hikes in Mount San Jacinto State Park for $5, and the first Friday of each month is free, except during special exhibitions.

Villagefest (323-8272). A farmers' market and street fair with live entertainment is held every Thursday evening along Palm Canyon Drive between Baristo and Tahquitz.

PALM SPRINGS

Near Palm Springs

Indian Canyons (325-5673). There are three magnificent canyons — Andreas, Murray and Palm — off of South Palm Springs Drive that all boast incredible views, towering cliffs and unparalleled beauty. Grab a picnic lunch and go for a hike.

Indian Wells Date Garden (74-774 Highway 111, 346-2914). A friendly shop in a little house along the highway. Take time to sit outside and sip on a date shake, or enjoy a scoop of date ice cream.

Joshua Tree National Monument (Take Hwy. 62 to Twentynine Palms, 367-7511). The Mojave Desert joins with the lower Colorado Desert to form this monument, which is approximately 1200 square miles, and a rock climber's paradise. $5 per car.

La Quinta Sculptureland (57-325 Madison St., in La Quinta, 564-6464). No, it's not a misplaced segment of Disneyland. It houses more than 300 sculptures by world-renowned artists, a lake, and rental golf carts for your viewing pleasure.

KEEP FIT-RECREATION

Palm Springs Athletic Club (543 S. Palm Canyon, 323-7722). Even on vacation, you will want to continue to look great. This extremely gay and lesbian friendly club has daily, weekly, monthly and seasonal passes.

EAT

Fine Dining

Shame on the Moon (69-950 Frank Sinatra Dr., 324-5515). An upscale, very gay place to claim a table for a couple of hours. Reservations are essential. $15-22.

The Wild Goose (67-938 Highway 111, Cathedral City, 328-5775). A popular, award-winning local spot, featuring wild game and fowl. It is especially famous for its duck dishes. Reservations recommended. $15-45.

Casual Dining

Blue Coyote Grill (445 N. Palm Canyon Dr., 327-1196). Trendy, southwestern cuisine in the heart of downtown. Try the charbroiled Yucatan lamb marinated in grapefruit juice and garlic, or the duck enchiladas in red tortillas with fig sauce. Great margaritas. $8-30.

El Gallito (68-820 Grove St., Cathedral City, 328-7794). One of the most authentic Mexican food restaurants in the valley. It's always crowded, but the enchiladas verdes and sopapillas are well worth the wait. $3-12.

Michael's (68-665 Highway 111, Cathedral City, 321-7197). Inexpensive local spot for scratch biscuits, delicious pancakes and biscuits and gravy that's to die for. Open for breakfast and lunch only. $2.50-10.

Native Foods (1775 E. Palm Canyon Dr., 416-0070). The only completely vegetarian restaurant in the valley is tucked in the Courtyard shops at the Smoke Tree Villa shopping strip, near the Bee Charmer Inn. Yummy stir fries, veggie lasagna and rice and bean dishes. $3-12.

Pepper Maggie's (42-245 Washington Blvd., Palm Desert, 360-6135). An imaginative diner featuring the foods of Central and South America. Two favorites are the traditional Spanish paella and the paradilla, which is an Argentinean grilled fillet. $7-15.

Rainbow Cactus Cafe (212 S. Indian Canyon Dr., 325-3868). Frequented by the local gay crowd, the food offerings are traditional diner fare: burgers, sandwiches and pastas. A pleasant place to relax. $7-15.

Red Tomato-House of Lamb (68-784 Grove St. at Hwy. 111, Cathedral City, 328-7518). The two restaurants under one roof dish up magnificent pizza and lamb entrees. And the owner, Bill, does all the cake and pie baking himself. $8-17.

Coffeehouses

Village Pride Coffeehouse (214 E. Arenas Rd., 323-9120). Cushy couches and pillows; great lesbian and gay card selection. Doesn't open until 10 a.m. daily. $1-5.

PALM SPRINGS

🎵 PLAY-MEET

Since the closing of **Delilah's** — which was the valley's only women's nightclub — a couple of other bars in Cathedral City have opened their doors to the lesbian community. The festive **DP Poolside Bar** (at Desert Palms Inn, 67-580 Hwy. 111, 324-3000 or 800/801-8696) hosts women's nights every Wednesday and Saturday. And **Sundance Saloon** (36-737 Cathedral Canyon Rd., 321-0031) invites two-stepping women into its country-western digs on Wednesday and Sunday nights.

💲 SHOP

General Shopping

Right in Palm Springs is the **Desert Fashion Plaza** (123 N. Palm Canyon Dr., 320-8282), which is anchored by Saks Fifth Avenue. Or just wander in and out of the unique shops, which can be pricey, along Palm Canyon Drive. Some of the bigger shopping areas are **Town Center** (Hwy. 111 at Monterey Ave., 346-2121) and **El Paseo Village** (off Hwy. 111) in the town of Palm Desert. While Town Center is a more traditional mall, El Paseo — affectionately known as the "Rodeo Drive of the Desert" — is an avenue dedicated to designer boutiques, home furnishing shops, galleries and popular restaurants. For golfing supplies, as well as good babe-watching, check out **Lady Golf** (42-412 Bob Hope Dr., Rancho Mirage, 773-4949), which carries a large stock of golf apparel and resort wear.

Food Markets

Jensen's Finest Foods (Sunrise Way at Tahquitz, 325-8282). Full-service market and bakery with farm-fresh quality produce, gourmet and specialty foods.

Nature's Express Natural Food Market and Cafe (555 S. Sunrise Way, 323-9487). An organic market and diner, it has everything you need for holistic shopping.

Secondhand Stores

Revivals (68929 Perez Rd., Unit K, Cathedral City, 328-1330). All proceeds go to the AIDS project. Good selection of lava lamps and Naugahyde furniture.

Pride Shopping

Gay Mart (305 E. Arenas, 320-0606). Clothing, jewelry, stickers and adult video rentals.

Bookstores

Celebration Books (210 E. Arenas, 416-9299). Another good source for pride shopping, it's the desert's only exclusive gay and lesbian bookstore, and features lectures, as well as a book-signing series.

Bloomsbury Books (555 S. Sunrise Way #105, 325-3862). Specializes in out-of-print gay and lesbian books, including signed and rare originals.

KIDS' STUFF

Oasis Water Park (1500 S. Gene Autry Trail, 325-7873). The park features the "Black Widow" water slide, as well as 15 other water attractions. Dive in!

Camelot Park Family Entertainment Center (67-700 E. Palm Canyon Dr., Cathedral City, 321-9893). Miniature golf, go-carts, bumper boats, video arcade and batting cages.

SPIRITUAL

Christ Chapel of the Desert (4707 E. Sunny Dr., 327-2795). A Christian gay and lesbian church.

Integrity of the Desert (324-1826). Gay and lesbian Episcopals.

Unity of Palm Springs (815 S. Camino Real, 325-7377).

PALM SPRINGS

RESOURCES

General Information

Palm Springs Visitor Information Center (2781 N. Palm Canyon Dr., 778-8418 or 800/34-SPRINGS, www.palmsprings.com).
Desert Business Association (www.desert-winds.com). A comprehensive resource for gay- and lesbian-owned businesses, as well as a calendar of events.

Media

Gay and Lesbian Live Radio Talk Show. On 1010-AM, Sundays, 4-6 p.m.
Desert Daily Guide (320-3237). A thorough gay and lesbian guide to valley events.
The Bottom Line (323-0552). A monthly magazine for the desert area's gay and lesbian community that's heavy on features.
Desert Sun (322-8889, www.desert-sun.com). Palm Springs's daily newspaper.

Festivals

International Film Festival (778-8979). In January, more than 60 of the newest films are shown at theaters throughout town.
Nabisco-Dinah Shore LPGA Major Championship (324-4546, www.nabiscodinahshore.com). You thought I would never mention it. The Mission Hills Country Club in Rancho Mirage hosts the world's greatest women golfers as they compete for the coveted major pro-am championship title. It's also a grand excuse for the gigantic women's party **LesboEXPO** (e-mail lesexpo@aol.com). With 15,000-20,000 extra lesbians in town, this party is held on a private estate, complete with beer, food, two pools and several spas. What are you waiting for?

Port Townsend, Washington

area code 360

WHAT TO EXPECT

Why do all the great lesbian coastal towns begin with a "P"? Provincetown, Port Townsend ... okay, I can only think of a couple very similar ones — both at the tip of impressive peninsulas. But while Provincetown is already established as a gay and lesbian resort, Port Townsend is about 25 years behind.

In the late 19th century, Port Townsend was expected to become the San Francisco-like metropolis of the north once it established itself as an important seaport. But because the end of the Great Northern Railroad line was in Seattle, Port Townsend never experienced the population boom that was expected, and has remained a small maritime community. It is famous for its Victorian architecture and now its growing tourist industry. In fact, more than 75 percent of Port Townsend's buildings are on the National Register of Historic Places and most of these have been converted into Bed & Breakfasts.

It is not just the abundance of cute accommodations, though, that lures travelers to the area. Even though parts of Washington's Olympic Peninsula receive more than 240 inches of rain per year, Port Townsend only gets 15-20 because it is situated in the Olympics's "rain shadow," a geographic region that is protected from severe weather patterns. Needless to say, a lot of dry, or at least semi-dry, days may be spent hiking, kayaking, digging "steamers" — the local term for clams — or lounging on one of the many sandy beaches.

For women who love the outdoors, Port Townsend can't be beat for its locale. It's a good place for kids, too. With Olympic National Park to the west, and the San Juan Islands northeast in Puget Sound, wilderness lies in every direction. From the San Juans, get on a boat and search for orca whales. Rent a bike and explore the grounds around Port Townsend. Drive to Hurricane Ridge in Olympic National Park for sunset. There are thousands of things to do. And be sure to pack binoculars because you won't want to miss any of the local wildlife.

With a population of 8,000, it seems that lesbians would stick out in Port Townsend like a sore thumb, but, unfortunately, they don't. That's because the town is socially integrated and culturally liberal enough that there isn't any one group of people that sticks out at all — except in the summer when the place is taken over by visiting musicians, writers and tourists. So, don't be surprised if you find yourself on Water Street wondering where all the lesbians are. Visit the Food Co-op on Lawrence Street, however, or the beach at Fort Worden State Park, and you will find yourself among the company of women. Guaranteed.

You won't find the great gay bars of Provincetown, nor the rainbow flags in every shop window. And fierce competition between lesbian B&Bs has yet to intensify. But give it a few years. Port Townsend has all the makings of a great lesbian resort area.

What To Bring

A hefty raincoat is a good idea, as well as a light-weight one since it's been known to mist continually for more than 24 hours. Also bring waterproof hiking boots and jeans that can get covered in mud, as well as beach wear for brilliant sunny days. Binoculars are a must.

Best Time To Visit

July is usually the driest month of the year.

Getting There

From Sea-Tac Airport, near Seattle, hop across the Puget Sound on **Port Townsend Airways** (800/385-6554) for $69 per person, one way. Owners John and Jenny will schedule a flight on demand, and are super flexible. For directions to Port Townsend via land, sea or air, check out this Web page: host.kolke.com/lizzies.map.html.

PORT TOWNSEND

Getting Around

Instead of flying into Port Townsend, another option is to rent a car from Sea-Tac Airport, which will allow greater mobility for visiting Olympic National Park, as well as other areas of the Olympic Peninsula.

STAY

Hotel

Palace Hotel (1004 Water St., 385-0773, or 800/962-0741). Every room in this elegant Victorian hotel is named after a "Miss So-and-so" — names left over from bawdier times. The beautiful rooms include breakfast. $65-185.

Guest Houses

Annapurna Inn (538 Adams St., 385-2909, or 800/868-2662). A vacation in itself, the retreat center provides "transformation to radiant health" via vegan cuisine, yoga, massage and steam baths. Nightly, $70-108; three-day package, $250.

Gaia's Getaway (4343 Hains St., 385-1194). A lesbian-owned, homey studio apartment. Comes with fully equipped kitchen and laundry facilities. Children and pets accepted. Nightly, $75; weekly, $350.

Ginger's Guest House (841 K St., 385-1587). One room in a private house, midway between downtown Port Townsend and Fort Worden State Park. A ramp entrance and all facilities on the first floor make this a good option for the physically challenged. Residents live on the second floor. $35-40.

Lizzie's (731 Pierce, 385-4168, or 800/700-4168). The hosts go out of their way to treat guests to a relaxing time. $85-135.

Ravenscroft Inn (533 Quincy St., 385-2784). A very lesbian-friendly Bed & Breakfast. Your morning meal will even be accompanied by a Steinway grand piano concert. $65.

Economy

Olympic Hostel (in Fort Worden State Park, 385-0655). You can't beat the location. Rooms are available for couples and families, and include blankets and pillows. The common room remains open all day. Sheets and towels may be rented. $12-15, with discounts given to cyclists.

SEE-DO

In and Around Port Townsend

Centrum Cultural Center (385-3102). Most of Port Townsend's summer cultural events are produced by this music and arts foundation housed at Fort Worden State Park. A sampling of events include Seattle Symphony concerts, the Port Townsend Writer's Conference, the Festival of American Fiddle Tunes and the annual Jazz Festival.

Fort Worden State Park (200 Battery Way, 385-4730). This is the only army fort to be named after a naval man, and at one time boasted the largest military post protecting the Puget Sound. The park has everything from the **Marine Science Center** (532 Battery Way, 385-5582), the **Rhododendron Garden**, and camping, to sandy beaches and hiking trails that overlook the Strait of Juan de Fuca. Watch for harbor seals in the surf along the coastline.

Jefferson County Historical Society Museum (210 Madison St., 385-1003). If history is your thing, visit this 1891 building featuring a jail, courtroom, fire department and historical displays detailing the area's formative years. Admission by donation.

Old Fort Townsend (On Route 20 four miles south of town, 385-3595). The old military fort-turned-state park houses an active bald eagle nesting site in a secluded portion of the park.

Olympic Music Festival (527-8839). During summer months, world-renowned guest artists play chamber music in a dairy barn near the town of Quilcene, only a few miles out of Port Townsend. Concerts are Saturdays and Sundays, mid-June to mid-September. Seats are

PORT TOWNSEND

available inside the barn, or buy a lawn ticket ($9) and spread out a picnic dinner.

Near Port Townsend

Dungeness Spit (near Sequim). This seven-mile natural sand jetty is always peaceful and, being in the "rain shadow" of the Olympics, hardly gets any rain. Wildlife that's often spotted along the shoreline are seals, sea lions and birds.

Fort Flagler State Park (385-1259). The fort is at the tip of Marrowstone Island, near Port Townsend, and is yet another former army post. An 18-mile bike ride from Port Townsend is one of the least hilly rides around. Rent bicycles at **Port Townsend Cyclery** (100 Tyler St., 385-6470).

Olympic National Park (600 E. Park Ave., Port Angeles, 452-4501). Parts of the park are so lush and overgrown that they are as yet uncharted. If you chose to drive around the Olympic Peninsula to the Pacific Coast, stop for lunch at the settlement of Sappho, about 40 miles west of Port Angeles on Highway 101. The gas station at the crossroads has the best split pea soup, and signs are posted throughout the store with quotes from many of Sappho's classical Greek love poems.

San Juan Islands (385-5288). Take a cruise to this gem. Once you arrive on the islands, stop by **Susie's Mopeds** (378-5244) one block up from the ferry landing, and rent a two-wheeler to cruise around. $15 per hour; $45 per day. Or catch a sightseeing boat or sea-kayaking trip into the water surrounding the islands, which is home to migrating orca whales. Boats depart regularly from both Port Townsend and the San Juans.

KEEP FIT-RECREATION

Port Townsend Athletic Club (229 Monroe St., 385-6560). A place to go on a very rainy day, offering aerobics, racquetball, weights, machines, Jacuzzi and sauna.

EAT

Fine Dining

Blackberries (385-9950). There are two locations for this unique Pacific Northwestern fare — one is in the Palace Hotel on Water Street. The other is on the grounds at Fort Worden State Park. Try the halibut-salmon braid dressed with native salal berries, or the New York strip coated with a whiskey cream sauce. $5-20.

Casual Dining

Aldrich's (940 Lawrence, 385-0500). A combination health food restaurant-gourmet grocery store. A place in which elegant European chocolates can compliment an abundant salad from the salad bar.

Coho Cafe (1044 Lawrence St., 379-1030). Healthy, eclectic cuisine and full-service juice and espresso bar. Breakfast served all day. Very lesbian friendly. $3-12.

Elevated Ice Cream (627 Water St., 385-1156). It's "elevated" in the sense that the company began serving its old-fashioned, homemade ice creams, sherbets and Italian ices from a streetside antique Victorian elevator cage with the slogan "Lift your spirits!"

Fountain Cafe (920 Washington St., 385-1364). The specialty is fresh, local seafood, such as mussels and clams with fresh basil and egg linguine in a garlic wine sauce, or the smoked salmon garnished with scotch and caviar. $4-15.

Khu Larb Thai (225 Adams St., 385-5023). Locals claim this is the best Thai food restaurant outside Seattle. The chicken satay and fresh seafood stew are best bets. $5-12.

Lighthouse Cafe (955 Water St., 385-1165). A diner-type setting with a view of Puget Sound. Try the homemade clam chowder or the seafood omelet. $3-8.

Silverwater Cafe (237 Taylor St., 385-6448). Everything is truly handmade, from the blue dinnerware to desserts. The owners will throw together a picnic basket for your day at the beach. $3-14.

Coffeehouses

Bread and Roses Bakery (230 Quincy St., 385-1044). Locals consider this the best place to get a morning treat and cup of strong, northwest coffee. $1-5.

SHOP

General Shopping

The main drag, Water Street, offers an abundance of antique stores, but what do you expect from a Victorian B&B haven? There are also a couple of choice women's clothing stores, **Kaleidoscope** (636 Waterfront Pl., 379-9225), and **About Time Fashions** (825 Water St., 385-4795).

Food Markets

Aldrich's (940 Lawrence, 385-0500). A medley of four food stores under one roof: Uncle Gary's Fresh Produce, Sally's Elegant Foods, Tom's Meat and Seafood, and Aldrich's Groceries from Around the World.

The Food Co-op (1033 Lawrence St., 385-2883). Full-line grocery store featuring organic produce, bulk herbs, macrobiotic supplies and foods for special dietary needs.

Secondhand Stores

Wild Thing (215 Tyler St., 379-9516). Definitely lives up to its name.

Pride Shopping

Phoenix Rising (839 Water St., 385-4464). Features women's jewelry, gems and bumper stickers.

Bookstores

Phoenix Rising (839 Water St., 385-4464). An anchor on the main street, with a huge selection of New Age and spiritual books, as well as feminist and children's literature. Also, New Age music, cards, posters and crystals.

KIDS' STUFF

Marine Science Center (532 Battery Way, 385-5582). Located on the pier at Fort Worden State Park, the nature center houses aquaria exhibits, touch tables, an underwater video camera, microscopes, marine skeletons and fossils, and maps and charts. Youth summer camps and art programs are also available.

SPIRITUAL

Religious Society of Friends-Quakers (385-7070). Worship is Sundays, 10 a.m. There is a potluck and discussion the last Friday of every month.

St. Paul's Episcopal Church (1020 Jefferson, 385-0770). Holy Communion is Sundays at 8 and 10 a.m., and Wednesdays at 10 a.m.

Unity Center of Port Townsend (620 Tyler St., 385-6519). Sunday service is 11 a.m.

RESOURCES

General Information

Port Townsend Visitor Information Center (2437 E. Sims Way, 385-2722, www.olympus.net/biz/ptchamber).

Women's Center (1334 Lawrence St., 385-2315). Has a full schedule of events and a library featuring more than 500 books. Call ahead for a quarterly newsletter. Also exhibits art works by women.

PORT TOWNSEND

Media

There is no gay or lesbian community publication, but the two local papers — **The Leader** (385-5100, www.olympus.net/biz/leader) and **Peninsula Daily News** (385-2335) — offer plenty of information about what to do during your stay. Check at the **Women's Center** for a newsletter and schedule of women-related events.

Festivals

Rhododendron Festival (385-1904). The third week of May. This annual celebration of the state flower is timed just right for the height of its blooming season. The festival features a craft fair, parade and the Rhodie Run. The Olympic Peninsula Chapter of The American Rhododendron Society holds its flower show at the chapel in Fort Worden State Park.

Wooden Boat Festival (385-3628). The town goes nuts for this week-long event the first week of September. More than 100 wooden boats are displayed in educational, historical and cultural settings. Festivities include exhibits, workshops, lectures, demonstrations and boat shop tours.

Provincetown, Massachusetts

area code 508

WHAT TO EXPECT

From the day that a lesbian comes out of the closet, it is a given — even written somewhere in the Lesbian Code of Ethics — that at some time in her life she will make a trip to Provincetown. Why? What beckons her to the tip of Cape Cod? It is so far away, and she had never even heard of the place before kissing another woman. In grade school, she never learned that the Pilgrims landed in Provincetown first, and *then* went on to Plymouth. Why wasn't that in the history books? Consequently, when she finally stands on three-mile-long Commercial Street looking up at Provincetown's Pilgrim Monument at the top of High Pole Hill, she knows it represents her and the long, yet direct, road she has taken to get there. The monument could have been built for her ancestors that stopped there 375 years ago, or for those who put the booming whaling commerce on the map in the early 19th century, or even for the evolving, turn-of-the-century summer artists' colony. The monument could even be for all gays and lesbians everywhere because we are Pilgrims, aren't we? When we first arrive on Commercial Street we celebrate knowing that we have arrived in the only town on earth where gay and lesbians are the majority.

The important thing to remember, though, is that Provincetown is a "town." Beneath all of its resort hoop-la — and its metamorphosis from summer's "Adventures in Lesbian La-La Land," to winter's "Lesbian Sleepy Hollow" — there is a wickedly beautiful place, and it's the kind of place that lesbian business owners like to promote. Contrary to popular belief, there is an act of nature happening at the tip of Cape Cod that involves other things besides lesbian mating calls. It's about watching: whales, birds, tides — all right, women, too. One of the most satisfying, if not unusual, things to do in Provincetown is to stroll down Commercial Street at 6:30 a.m. Only a few other souls have batted an eye at that hour. Slip into the Provincetown General Store for a cappuccino-to-go — most likely the only place in town that will be open — and continue west toward the beach to catch an early morning salty breeze. Or straddle your rented mountain bike and cycle toward the north beach on trails surrounding the dunes. Or grab a bucket and harvest cranberries from the low-lying bogs across Highway 6 toward the dunes and Race Point Beach. And if you have already done all of those things, take a whale-watching excursion that leaves early in the morning from the piers at Commercial and Standish Streets, though whaling season is generally during the summer.

Then, after spending the day frolicking in nature, return to the Pied Piper or Vixen and dance yourself silly. Tomorrow, do it all over again. It makes for long days, but there are a lot of things to do in Provincetown, whether there are thousands of other tourists around or not.

What To Bring

If you are going to the beach in the summer, jeans, a sweater or a sweatshirt are nice because the breeze, especially in the early morning, can be nippy. The rest of the day in town can be casual: shorts and a T-shirt. Dress up a little for dinner. Be sure to pack a raincoat any time of the year.

Best Time To Visit

Shopkeepers and innkeepers are trying to entice visitors to Provincetown year-round: as a Thanksgiving getaway, or as a quiet, mid-winter retreat. However, **Women's Week** (487-4966) in late October is the prime time to view autumn colors, as well as witness women taking over the place.

Getting There

It's an easy two-and-a-half hour drive from Boston on I-93 south to

PROVINCETOWN

Route 3, then east and north on Route 6. If you have more time, take scenic Route 6A along the coast through old Cape Cod towns.

Cape Cod Air (800/352-0714) leaves Boston three to five times a day for Provincetown for $79-139 round trip, depending on the season. The **Plymouth and Brockton Bus Line** (746-0378) operates year round and stops at each town between Provincetown and Hyannis, with hourly connections between Hyannis and Logan International Airport. And, finally, the **Bay State Cruise** (617/723-7800) leaves Boston for Provincetown once a day from May through October. One way on the ferry is $18; round trip is $30.

Getting Around

Taxis can be called at bus, boat and plane terminals, or from anywhere, for that matter. The **Provincetown Trolley** (487-9483) conducts 40-minute guided tours through town and along the National Seashore. The trolley leaves from Commercial Street outside Town Hall every half hour from April to October.

STAY

Motel

The Moors Motel (59 Provinceland Rd., 800/842-6379). A woman-owned motel at the west end of town offering spectacular sunsets and walks on the beaches. $80-120.

Guest Houses

Many of these guest houses do not accept credit cards. Be sure to bring enough cash or travelers' checks to pay for accommodations, and inquire about the method of payment when making reservations. All of the following are woman-owned:

Bradford Gardens Inn (178 Brad ford St., 487-1616 or 800/432-2334). Spacious rooms with fireplaces and antiques. Large cottages. One of the original lesbian-owned guest houses in Provincetown. $69-185.

Check'er Inn Resort (25 Winthrop St., 487-9029 or 800/894-9029). Homemade breakfast in common room with a fireplace and piano. Jacuzzi in a plant-filled sun room. Sun decks, lawn and gardens, on-site parking. Women only. $90-150.

Dexter's Inn (6 Conwell St., 487-1911). Unique clusters of clean, comfortable, smoke-free rooms. Continental breakfast is served on the flower garden patio. Centrally located. $75-95.

Dusty Miller Inn (82 Bradford St., 487-2213). Named after the silver-leafed plant that grows wild on Cape Cod sand dunes, the inn has every kind of accommodation: old Victorian rooms in the main house, motel-like rooms in the recent expansion, and two efficiency apartments. $68-115.

Fairbanks Inn (90 Bradford St., 487-0386 or 800/324-7265). A warm and inviting, magnificently restored 1770s sea captain's home offering antique-filled rooms, fireplaces, and four poster and canopied beds. $65-120.

Gabriel's (104 Bradford St., 487-3232). Gabriel was the first to open a women's guest house in Provincetown. Now, she offers everything a girl could possibly want: hot tub, steam room, sauna, library, kitchen, garden and sun deck, as well as Siren's Workshops, which are a variety of classes focusing on the health of the body, mind and spirit, collectively. $75-125.

Gull Walk Inn (300-A Commercial St., 487-9027 or 800/309-4725). Six rooms that include a Continental breakfast. Kids and pets welcome. Women only. $45-65.

Halle's (14 W. Vine St., 487-6310). Cottage and apartments with outside entrances in quiet West End, one block from the harbor. $80-95. A townhouse rents for $800 by the week only.

Hargood House at Bayshore (493 Commercial St., 487-9133). Waterfront views, some with fireplaces, private beach and decks. Open all year. $90-195.

Heritage House (7 Center St., 487-3692). Charming 19th Century home with views of Cape Cod Bay from its verandah. Friendly owners. $65-85.

Lady Jane's Inn (7 Central St., 487-3387). Located one-half block

PROVINCETOWN

from the bay near shops and galleries. All rooms have full private baths. $90.

Lavender Rose (186 Commercial St., 487-6648). Situated in the thick of all the downtown action, the inn features a Continental breakfast, as well as a 10-percent discount on all entrees in its Cactus Garden Restaurant. $85-125.

Plums B&B (160 Bradford St., 487-2283). The innkeeper of this old whaling captain's five-room Victorian house tries to sit down and chat with her guests every morning during a gourmet breakfast, and has been doing so for thirteen years. Five rooms, all with private bath. Women only. $99.

Ravenwood Guest House (462 Commercial St., 487-3203). Year-round, fully equipped efficiencies, penthouse and apartments. It is only a ten-minute walk to center of town through the gallery district. Two different apartments, $675-850 per week; the guest room is $546 per week; and a one-bedroom, free-standing condo cottage is $850 per week. There is a seven-night minimum during July and August.

Rose Acre (5 Center St., 487-2347). A somewhat secluded place, compared to the others. Rose Acre is tucked down a private drive behind the Heritage House and has the unhurried atmosphere of a sprawling Cape house. Women only. $90.

Tucker Inn (12 Center St., 487-0381). A stately looking inn a half-block from the town center. $80-100.

White Wind Inn (174 Commercial St., 487-1526). A lovely, white Victorian circa 1845. The suite on the top floor has two decks and an unblocked view of the whole town. $105-180.

Windamar House (568 Commercial St., 487-0599). Located in the quiet east end with some rooms overlooking Cape Cod Bay. $60-110.

SEE-DO

In and Around Provincetown

Bird-watching. In the spring, migrating hawks and songbirds are pushed off course by the wind and collect in great numbers in Beech

Forest, located on Race Point Road. In the fall, keep an eye on the town dump for hawks, eagles and vultures, as well as rare species of gulls.

Cape Cod National Seashore (349-3785). Forty miles of waterfront stretches from Provincetown along the east side of the Cape. Pick up hiking and bicycling trail maps at the **Province Lands Visitor's Center** (at Race Point Beach, 487-1256), which is north of the town center.

Center for Coastal Studies (59 Commercial St., 487-3622). The Center is internationally known for its extensive research on the whales found in the area. Open year round for research and education.

Fine Arts Works Center (24 Pearl St., 487-9960). Each winter, nine-month residencies are offered to selected young writers and artists who offer presentations of their work on Saturday nights throughout their stay.

Pilgrim Monument and Museum (1 High Pole Rd., 487-1310). The granite structure commemorates the landing of the Pilgrims in Provincetown in November 1620, before they reached Plymouth. The lung-busting climb to the top is worth the view.

Provincetown Art Association and Museum (460 Commercial St., 487-1750). Four galleries displaying historic and contemporary area artists.

Provincetown Heritage Museum (356 Commercial St., 487-7098). Permanent exhibits tell about Provincetown's whaling and fishing industries, and the summer art colony that began in 1899.

Whale-watching. Whale-watching boats leave Macmillan Pier and Fisherman's Wharf frequently between April and October. Along with humpback, right and finback whales, the area is teeming with dolphins.

KEEP FIT-RECREATION

Bicycling Province Land Trails. There are approximately eight miles of path, including a five-mile loop through the dunes and other detours to Race Point Beach and Herring Cove Beach.

Provincetown Gym (170 Commercial St., 487-2776). Woman-owned and offering daily, weekly and monthly punch cards.

PROVINCETOWN

EAT

Fine Dining

Mews (429 Commercial St., 487-1500). The original location got its name from the Old English word meaning "a stable behind a king's castle." It is now an elegant eatery on the waterfront. $14-35.

Martin House (157 Commercial St., 487-1327). This local favorite whips up a satisfying feast of vegetarian feijoada, stuffed loin of spring rabbit, porterhouse steak, and goat cheese soufflé. $14-30.

Red Inn (15 Commercial St., 487-0050). The food is as simple as the name, yet original and delicious. Specialty is a redux of classic Cape Cod seafood cuisine. $11-25.

Casual Dining

A&P Salad Bar (Shank Painter Rd., 487-4903). If all that you crave is a bountiful salad, then visit Provincetown's biggest supermarket. $2-10, depending on how carried away you get.

Ciro and Sals (4 Kiley Court, 487-0049). A traditional Italian diner specializing in seafood dishes. $8-24.

Dodie's Diner (401-1/2 Commercial St., 487-3868). Try a "Shore Dinner" to go — twin lobsters, clam chowder, steamed clams and corn on the cob — and head to the beach. $4-20.

Lobster Pot (321 Commercial St., 487-0842). Here, the customers, and the lobsters, are queens — in more ways than one. You can have your clawed friends sliced, diced, or served on a gold platter — any way you like 'em. Woman-owned. $12-29.

Lorraine's (229-R Commercial St., 487-6074). Authentic Mexican food direct from Lake Tahoe, California. Lorraine has found a mouthwatering way to combine her third generation Mexican culinary traditions with New England ingredients. Woman-owned. $5-15.

Napi's (7 Freeman St., 487-1145). Originally a Greek diner, Napi's has evolved to include a variety of fresh seafood and pasta dishes, such as asparagus ravioli. Whole wheat bread is baked daily. Smoke-free environment. $12-41.

Café Crudité (336 Commercial St. #6, in the Pilgrim House complex, 487-6237). A wholesome vegetarian restaurant that is a little more on the affordable side. Open for breakfast. $2-7.

The Flagship (463 Commercial St., 487-4200). Chef Polly offers a creative twist to fresh seafood and vegetarian fare. Harbor views and live entertainment. Lesbian-owned. $11-30.

The Moors (Bradford St. west extension, 487-0840). Famous for its Portuguese menu featuring *espada cozida* and *porco em pau*, as well as baked stuffed lobster and prime rib. $12-25.

Coffeehouses

Provincetown General Store (147 Commercial St., 487-0300). Stroll west on Commercial Street in the early morning, and this will be one of the only places open. Cappuccinos and fresh muffins.

🎵 PLAY-MEET

Pied Piper Lounge (193-A Commercial St., 487-1527). Provincetown's oldest women's bar is sometimes frequented by gay men, but not always. The place rocks on Saturday afternoons during the Tea Dance.

Vixen (336-A Commercial St., 487-6424). Women's lounge and bar located at the Pilgrim House.

Zax (67 Shank Painter Rd., 487-3122). It's generally a men's bar, but Sunday is "Women's Night."

💰 SHOP

Food Markets

A&P (Shank Painter Rd., 487-4903). It's not just a regular grocery store. In the autumn, the produce section stocks at least eleven varieties of pears!

PROVINCETOWN

Galleries

Berta Walker Gallery (208 Bradford St., 487-6411). A woman-owned gallery featuring several Provincetown women artists.

Ellen Harris Gallery East (355 Commercial St., 487-1414). The collection runs the gamut of mediums: paintings, sculptures, ceramics, glass, you name it.

Julie Heller Gallery (2 Gosnold St., 487-2169). In addition to an assortment of early Provincetown paintings, the collection also includes antique and estate jewelry, and commitment rings.

Passions Gallery (336 Commercial St. #2, 487-5740). Open by appointment year-round, this is a serious collection of woman-oriented art.

Pride Shopping

Pride's of Provincetown (182 Commercial St., 487-1127). Lesbian and gay pride merchandise.

Sand Castles by the Sea (234 Commercial St., 487-4346). Gay and lesbian pride products, and a whole lot more.

Womencrafts (376 Commercial St., 487-2501). The quintessential lesbian department store. All they need are blue-light specials. There is a 5-percent lesbian discount. Go on, prove it!

Cape Card (230 Commercial St., 487-2029). Gifts and cards, not necessarily lesbian-oriented, but a good selection nonetheless.

Clothing

Diane Z (273 Commercial St., 487-0030). A boutique for today's woman featuring Girbaud, Calvin Klein and Dr. Maartens. And there is a 10-percent cash discount for women.

Bookstores

Recovering Hearts Bookstore (4 Standish St., 487-4875). A great selection of contemporary books: lesbian, women's studies, New Age, recovery, as well as best sellers. The owners might barter with you for some purchases.

🦋 KIDS' STUFF

Provincetown has activities for kids of all ages: playing on the beaches and sand dunes, renting bicycles, whale-watching, touring the harbor by boat, climbing to the top of Pilgrim Monument, sailing and wind surfing lessons, and parasailing. For child care services, call the **Council on Aging** (487-9906).

☀ SPIRITUAL

St. Mary of the Harbor, Episcopal (487-2622).
St. Peter the Apostle, Catholic (487-0095).
United Methodist Church (487-0584 or 487-4925).
Universalist-Unitarian Meeting House (236 Commercial St., 487-9344).

☎ RESOURCES

General Information

Provincetown Chamber of Commerce (487-3424 or 800/637-8696, www.capecodaccess.com).
Helping Our Women (487-4357). A non-profit resource and referral center for women with chronic and life-threatening illness.

Media

***Provincetown* magazine** (487-1000). An arts and entertainment magazine published weekly from April to October.
Provincetown Advocate (487-1170). The publication most people turn to, though not necessarily gay-oriented.
Provincetown Banner (487-7400). Local news and features, distributed every Wednesday.

Santa Fe, New Mexico

area code 505

WHAT TO EXPECT

Santa Fe, like New Orleans, is one of the few American cities whose culture is so other-worldly that being there really takes you to an entirely different place and time. Perhaps that feeling comes from a bite of dry-roasted chipolte salsa — the likes of which you've never tasted before, or feeling the cool mustiness inside a 17th century adobe Spanish mission, or partaking in an ancient corn dance at one of the 18 Indian pueblos still in operation around the area.

In many ways, Santa Fe is like a misplaced European city. Its narrow, winding roads are reminiscent of an old Spanish village, and throngs of people and cars — especially during the summer — crowd its corridors. A labyrinth of hidden passageways and courtyards hint at intricate, age-old city plans and beg for exploration. Stairways lead nowhere, and alleys bustle with coffee shops and artist studios.

Santa Fe may be old — one of the oldest settlements in the U.S. — but it is not antiquated. Much of what the city offers has been common knowledge for thousands of years, and people still seek out its medicine. While many tourists believe Santa Fe is trendy and overpriced, and women who have settled in the state capital know the city seldom offers more than waitressing as a career, it is a small price to pay in order to indulge in the ancient spirituality of the place. Seven centuries ago the Pueblo Indians established a village named "dancing ground of the sun" on the site of what is now known as Santa Fe, and they believed that everything — mountains, wildlife, the sun and even corn meal — had a spirit of its own. Now, the majority of Santa Feans, and visitors as well, are taken in by the spiritual powers that the surrounding Pueblos still attribute to their land. There are dances, fiestas, carnivals, art shows ... every kind of imaginable celebration for the earth, its fruits and colors.

Lesbians, of course, are not exempt from Santa Fe's spiritual community. In fact, they are all one in the same, since the requirement to live anywhere near Santa Fe is to have some sort of intact spiritual belief system. Although Santa Fe does not have a lesbian "neighborhood," so to speak, there is no need for one. The city is small enough — 60,000 people — to easily pick out the lesbian crowd. Walk down the casual Guadalupe Street and when a lesbian drives by and takes notice, she will yell to you that you should meet her and her friends at the lesbian friendly Zia Diner. Or ask the barista at the Galisteo News coffeeshop what's happening in the community that weekend, and perhaps you will be invited to a party. The social key is to hang out on the informal, younger west side of town, rather than the trendy, expensive, established east end — unless you are looking to buy art.

Maybe it is the famous sunsets, or the colors of the red desert dotted with light-green sagebrush that attracts these women. Or it might be the lack of industry and the 7000-foot altitude that offers a wholesome alternative to big-city life. Whatever the reason for the current lesbian migration to the southwest, all those women can't be wrong.

What To Bring

A sleeveless, blue-denim work shirt is appropriate with a short skirt, cowboy boots and sunscreen. A straw hat is also useful under the hot sun.

Best Time To Visit

Santa Fe is a perfect place to visit any time of year. Even beneath the scorching, dry July sun a breeze at 7000-feet elevation has a cooling effect. In the summer, plan for afternoon thunderstorms and avoid the *arroyos*, which are dry river beds. They fill up fast in a deluge.

SANTA FE

Getting There

From the Albuquerque airport, either rent a car and drive northeast to Santa Fe (55 miles), or hop on a shuttle. If money is no object, fly directly into Santa Fe. It's not a major airport, so it's pricier.

Getting Around

There is too much broken glass along the streets to make cycling worthwhile. Therefore, if you are staying outside the downtown area, the best bet is to rent a car.

STAY

Guest Houses

Hummingbird Ranch (471-2921). Seven miles west of town on Route 10, is a welcoming, lesbian-owned ranch where you can breathe sage-scented air and enjoy the three Hs — hummingbirds, horses and humans. $100 for the casita.

Inn of the Turquoise Bear (342 E. Buena Vista St., 983-0798 or 800/396-4104). A gay-owned Bed & Breakfast housed in gay poet and Chinese translator Witter Bynner's renovated estate. In the 1920s, writer Mabel Dodge Luhan accused Bynner of introducing homosexuality to the state of New Mexico, after witnessing his outrageous pageants around the neighborhood wearing only a silk kimono. It's located six blocks from the downtown Plaza, and if you don't stay there, at least stop by between 5-7 p.m. for a complimentary glass of wine and tour of the grounds. The owners will talk your ears off. Children welcome. Eleven rooms. $80-120.

Open Sky (134 Turquoise Trail; 471-3475 or 800/244-3475). Located 10 minutes south of Santa Fe along the Turquoise Trail, a lesbian-owned, sprawling adobe complex where magnificent sunsets will revitalize your spirits. $70-120.

Triangle Inn (Route 11, Arroyo Cuyamungue; 455-3375). The ultimate, sprawling adobe compound, north of the Santa Fe Opera House. Luxurious private casitas. Lesbian-owned, with exclusively lesbian and gay clientele. $80-130. Pets are welcome for an additional $5 per night.

Camping

ARF (989-8627). This is a good chunk of lesbian-owned land north of town, against the foot of the Sangre de Cristos. Probably the most inexpensive accommodation in town, camping is available for a donation. Call ahead for directions — it's easy to get lost on the back roads through the sagebrush. Children and dogs are welcome.

SEE-DO

In and Around Santa Fe

Art Show Openings. Throughout the summer there are at least 12 gallery openings every Friday between 5-7 p.m. All of them are listed in Friday's "Pasatiempo" section of the Santa Fe *New Mexican* newspaper, but there's no need to carry the paper around with you. Just stroll around the Plaza area, or along Cañon Road, until you find a vociferous group of people drinking wine. Then, meander a few blocks with the whole gang to the next gallery.

Atalaya Trail. Also known as the "mountain-bike-junkie" trail. Five minutes from downtown, the trailhead at St. John's College campus eases into the Arroyos de los Chamisos neighborhood, then climbs into the Atalaya Mountains. All this, and the occasional peek into the backyards of the rich and possibly famous, who have built custom adobe castles along the hillsides.

Canyon Road (from Paseo de Peralta to Alemeda Ave.). Probably the longest strip of art galleries and studios in the west. Bring big bucks. Art is pricey in these parts.

Fenn Gallery (1075 Paseo de Peralta, 982-4631). The gallery also passes as a museum of early Taos and Santa Fe painters. Plan to spread out a picnic lunch in the sculpture garden.

Georgia O'Keefe Museum (217 Johnson St., 995-0785). The long-awaited collection of the artist's paintings and memorabilia has finally come into fruition. $5.

Loretto Chapel (219 Old Santa Fe Trail, 984-7971). Its "Miraculous Staircase" leading to the choir loft could be one of the wonders of the world. Try figuring out for yourself how it was built without nails, or central support.

Museum of Fine Arts (On the Plaza, 827-4455). There are always a few Georgia O'Keefe's on display, as well as R.C. Gorman's in the sculpture garden.

Palace of the Governors (100 Palace Ave., 827-6483). The oldest government building in continuous use in the U.S. is also New Mexico's historical museum.

Santa Fe Opera (986-5900). When the opera was founded in 1957, New Mexicans chose Santa Fe for its location because larger cities "have plenty of rain, mosquitoes, and a great deal of airplanes overhead." The opera house is situated in a large natural bowl in the Tesuque hills seven miles north of the city. Its season opens in early July and runs until the end of August.

Ten Thousands Waves (on Hyde Park Rd., 982-9304). A decadent, Japanese-style bath house, with massages, saunas, herbal wraps, Ayurvedic treatments and rejuvenating facials in which to indulge. Women's community bath hours are 12-8 p.m. everyday. $13-120.

Near Santa Fe

Abiquiu. Tours of painter Georgia O'Keefe's great house in Abiquiu, 35 miles northwest of Santa Fe, can be arranged by calling the **O'Keefe Foundation** (685-4539). There is also another way to experience the small town of Abiquiu: Clarisa Pinkola Estés — author of *"Women Who Run With The Wolves"* — offers women's retreats at O'Keefe's **Ghost Ranch** (call Maven Productions, 303/443-5858 or 800/813-1376).

Bandelier National Monument (14 miles north of Los Alamos on NM-4, 672-3861). Nowhere else is Willa Cather's idea of "vulval typography" more noticeable than in the canyons of Bandelier, home of the Anasazis — the cliff dwellers. Here, there are hikes into pink cavernous sandstone enclaves that are continually rounded and hollowed into a landscape that Cather deemed truly feminine. Don't just take the two-mile hike that loops around the visitor's center. It's best to indulge in a three-day backpack into this sacred land's remote areas. Be prepared to pack in all of your own water. Located 46 miles northwest of Santa Fe.

Bosque del Apache National Wildlife Refuge (16 miles south of Socorro on I-25, 835-1828). Thousands of blue herons, sandhill cranes, hawks and eagles migrate through this swampy area of the Rio Grande River every November and December. Lucky bird-watchers will enjoy the rare sighting of a whooping crane.

Bradbury Science Museum in Los Alamos (15th and Central Aves., Los Alamos, 667-4444). Displays modern nuclear and atomic weapons, as well as artifacts pertaining to the history and development of the atomic bomb. It sounds like a gruesome trip into an unpleasant segment of U.S. history, but it's one of the best science museums.

Tour the Wineries. Santa Fe and the surrounding cities of Los Alamos and Albuquerque are the hub of southwestern wine production. Although the grapes are grown further south near Las Cruces, several retired nuclear engineers from nearby Los Alamos have taken to preparing and selling their own libations. If a retired nuclear scientist can prepare a bottle of wine, it ought to be decent. A map of the area's wineries can be picked up at the Santa Fe Convention and Visitors Bureau, 201 W. Marcy Street.

KEEP FIT-RECREATION

Santa Fe Community College Rec. Center (S. Richards Ave., 438-1615). This is the definitive women's workout spot.

Fort Marcy (490 Washington Ave., 984-6725). And if there aren't any women at the Santa Fe Community College, they are at Fort Marcy, probably because the pool is bigger.

SANTA FE

EAT

Fine Dining

Geronimo (724 Canyon Rd., 982-1500). A popular, creatively simple American Southwestern cafe. Begin with lobster spring rolls, and continue with asiago veal. Lesbian friendly. $10-25.

Vanessie (434 W. San Francisco, 982-9966). This elegant restaurant is situated down a dark street, but don't shy away. It *is* lesbian-owned and serves up wild game, steak and seafood. If it's too pricey, come back later for dessert and a few tunes at the piano bar. $12-32.

Casual Dining

Cowgirl Hall of Fame (319 Guadalupe Street, 982-2565). Women gather here on a regular basis. Sit on bar stools made from tractor seats in a room with wall-to-wall cowgirl art. Even the bathroom's toilet-paper dispenser has a cowgirl motif. Especially known for its kids's menu and play area. $5-12.

Dave's Not Here (1115 Hickox Street, 983-7060). A popular hangout for lesbians, Dave sold his cafe a number of years back, but he left behind his designer hamburgers. $4-9.

Marisco's La Playa (537 W. Cordova, 982-2790). Seafood prepared à la Mexico. Try some shrimp or fish tacos and a *cerveza*. $5-15.

Santa Fe Baking Company (504 W. Cordova, 988-4292). Where the hip meet to sip, as well as nibble on delicious bacon and egg breakfast burritos. Open for breakfast and lunch only. Very lesbian friendly. $3-12.

Tomasita's (500 S. Guadalupe St., 983-5721). A local favorite for a chile fix. Both the red and green chiles are cooked fresh daily and have a defiant kick to them. Add your name early to the waiting list, or you will be eating a very late meal. $5-12.

Zia Southwest Diner (326 S. Guadalupe Street, 988-7008). A high energy, health conscious, American restaurant. Very gay and lesbian friendly. $3-15.

Coffeehouses

Dana's After Dark (222 N. Guadalupe, 982-5225). One of the only coffee shops in town that's open between 12-4 a.m. In fact, it doesn't even open until 6 p.m. A fun place to visit after a night on the town. It's not only lesbian friendly, but everybody friendly.

Downtown Subscription (376 Garcia Street; 983-3085). Along with racks of magazines to peruse, from "Out" to "Outside," the clientele is as fun to read as the international newspapers, and they allow dogs, as well.

El Cañon (in the Hilton Hotel at 308 W. San Francisco, 986-6417). It's more of a fancy dessert place to take a date. Popular with the lesbian crowd. Try "Flights," which is a grouping of wine samples.

Galisteo News (201 Galisteo Street; 984-1316). Extremely touristy, as it is smack downtown. Thursday nights there is a gays, lesbians and friends coffeehouse, 7-10 p.m.

Piano Bars

Vanessie (434 W. San Francisco, 982-9966). The bar draws the older, jazzy, elegant straight crowd. But because it is lesbian-owned, it also attracts some swanky gays and lesbians.

La Casa Seña (125 E. Palace Ave., 988-9232). Many of the professional singing waiters and waitresses also perform at the Santa Fe Opera. Desserts are $3-7.

The Old House (in the Eldorado Hotel, 309 W. San Francisco St., 988-4455). An elegant afternoon hangout for lesbians, not just for the social aspect, but for the relaxing atmosphere. $3-10.

♫ PLAY-MEET

The Drama Club (125 N. Guadalupe, 988-4374). Caters to gays and lesbians, with a mixed crowd showing up on the weekends because of the awesome DJs.

SANTA FE

💲 SHOP

General Shopping

Trader Jack's Flea Market (on Highway 285 seven miles north of Santa Fe, next to the Opera House). This is a no-cost Santa Fe art show cum garage sale, usually accompanied by a mariachi band. The best time to go is early Saturday morning, though it's open Friday through Sunday.

Palace of the Governors (At the downtown Plaza). Along the outside wall of the old government building Native Americans sell their wares of turquoise rings, pottery and Kachina dolls.

Sanbusco Market (500 Montezuma, 989-9390). Home to a variety of specialty shops, as well as the weekend farmer's market.

Food Markets

The Market Place (627 W. Alameda, 984-2852). A woman-owned natural food store.

Wild Oats (1090 St. Francis Dr., 983-5333). So many women in the aisles! Also, stop by the smaller store at 1708 Llano (473-4943).

Bookstores

Full Circle Books (2205 Silver SE, Albuquerque, 266-0022, www.bookgrrls.com/fcb). When passing through Albuquerque, stop in at the grandmother of New Mexico women's bookstores.

Garcia Street Books (376 Garcia St., 986-0151). A small store with a large selection of southwestern regional, poetry, art and architecture books.

Railyard (340 Read St., 995-0533). A favorite lesbian, feminist and children's bookstore. Sink into a cozy sofa by the fireplace, or strike up a conversation with the friendly staff.

She Said (in De Vargas Mall at Paseo de Peralta and St. Francis, 986-9196). Fairly new to the women's bookstore scene, this shop is stuffed to the gills with lesbian artifacts.

The Ark (133 Romero St., 988-3709). This somewhat hard-to-find bookstore has the largest collection of New Age and spiritual books, as well as gifts, jewelry and crystals.

KIDS' STUFF

Santa Fe Children's Museum (1050 Old Pecos Trail, 989-8359). An endless day of hands-on experiences, including a pseudo rock-climbing wall. $1.50-2.50.

Capt. Kid Toys (118 Don Gaspar, 982-TOYS; or 333 Montezuma, 988-CAPT). Two locations for lesbians who have children, and children who are gay and lesbian. And if you tell a joke, you will win a prize.

SPIRITUAL

Celebration (in the auditorium of the New Mexico School for the Deaf, near Cerillos Road and St. Francis Drive). The ideal place to witness the eclectic Santa Fe community. Every Sunday at 10:30 a.m. folks gather to get jazzed about life. People read anything from novels-in-progress to excerpts from the "Kama Sutra." A woman recently discussed the meaning of the word "Wow," which was followed by a rendition of "The Impossible Dream," sung by a tenor from the Santa Fe Opera. There is a good usually a good lesbian turnout.

RESOURCES

General Information

Santa Fe Convention and Visitors Bureau (201 W. Marcy St., 984-6760).

Lesbian Hotline (982-3301).

Women's Wednesday Night Group (438-8503 or wwng@aol.com). Meets at the Railyard Bookstore once a week. Call for a newsletter.

SANTA FE

Media

Out! (243-2540, www.swcp.com/~outmag). New Mexico's gay, lesbian and bisexual magazine, published in Albuquerque. Though most of the news and features are Albuquerque-oriented, it's a good place to start to find out what's happening. Pick up a copy at Galisteo News, both Wild Oats natural foods grocery stores and the Drama Club.

Out, Loud & Proud. Santa Fe radio talk show for gay and lesbian topics, Sundays, 10-11 a.m., KVSF 1260-AM; hosted by the same women who own the Triangle Inn.

Women's Voices (875-0112). Primarily focused on the Albuquerque women's community, this monthly newspaper lists art discussion groups, and other events in the area.

Gay Talk Radio. Sundays at 10 a.m. on KVSF-AM 1260.

Festivals

Zozobra Fiesta. The annual harvest-time burning of Old Man Gloom, the weekend after Labor Day in September, though not a lesbian event, is an opportunity to get all the things you ever wanted to yell at a man out of your system. You are screaming, "Burn him! Burn him!" and among fireworks and flames, you watch the huge, white puppet, meet his demise. And, hey, it's free.

Wiminfest (255-7274). Albuquerque Women's Music Festival on Memorial Day weekend. Tickets are available at Full Circle Books in Albuquerque.

Solstice (877-7245). The lesbian summer solstice celebration focuses on women's spirituality and Goddess consciousness. It takes place in the hills above the town of Jemez Springs. Lots of frolicking and hoopla, lesbian-festival style.

Tucson, Arizona

area code 520

WHAT TO EXPECT

Flying over Tucson, it's hard to imagine there is any life out there in the desert; it is so unbelievably dry. From the air, giant Saguaro cacti look like candelabras, and cover hill and dell of Tucson's five surrounding mountain ranges; their dull green pinnacles fade into an arid, dirty brown landscape. What could possibly attract so many women to the area? But lo! A river runs through it. The Santa Cruz River cuts through the downtown area — a welcome sight for thirsty eyes, just as it was for 17th century Pima Indians who founded "Stjukshon," meaning "spring at the foot of a black mountain," referring to a watering hole along the river.

Evidently, gallons and gallons of water from the river have quenched the thirst of many a settler, as the small Indian village has exploded into a major metropolis, making Tucson a desert oasis with skyscrapers, a state university, a politically progressive spirit in an otherwise conservative state, a flourishing lesbian community, and a thriving arts community. No other Arizona city can boast all of those things, which makes Tucson an ideal lesbian vacation destination; you just have to get off the plane to see that it is anything but dried up.

Most of your "city" time — versus "desert" time — will probably be spent strolling along Fourth Avenue between the University of Arizona and the downtown area, seeking out a tasty tamale stand, a lesbian-frequented coffee shop, ice cream, or a place to sit and soak up the sun. Among the street's many boutiques and used clothing and record shops is the high-profile bookstore Antigone. For a women's bookstore it is a sight to behold. Not only is it the premier Fourth Avenue bookstore — unlike most cities' women's bookstores that are in the suburbs — but it is huge and exudes lesbian energy. Of course, it helps that the gay and lesbian community center, Wingspan, is directly across the street, which is yet another anomaly. Check out its lending library — if there is something you wish to borrow, take it home and mail it back.

Another bookstore, Girlfriends, is quickly becoming "Lesbian Central" in the northwest part of town, the neighborhood in which most lesbians live. When the owners installed a dance floor, it was just the thing to keep the place buzzing as a bookstore and coffeeshop by day, and a bar and dance club by night. And there is the more upscale lesbian bar Ain't Nobody's Biz northeast of downtown, placing the three lesbian hangouts in the shape of a triangle. You can't get more gay than that.

You won't want to spend all of your time in town, however. The desert beckons, and any route leading out of Tucson will be correct for finding hiking trails and picnic areas. Plan ahead, though. It's not fun to trail blaze through cactus forests without educating yourself first about which of the prickly species will attack you, such as the jumping cholla. Therefore, the first place to visit should be the Arizona-Sonora Desert Museum. The museum fenced off a nice tract of land and erected signs pointing to particular animals and plants, and explaining how they exist in their natural habitat. The end result is an *au naturale*, roofless, educational and entertaining wonderland that's not to be missed. It's much like the feeling you get in all of Tucson. You will leave the area with an appreciation for desert life that you weren't aware existed.

What To Bring

Most Tucsonian women wear shorts and "summer" clothes year-round, but if you plan on dressing up a bit, the usual attire is jeans, a crisp shirt and cowgirl boots.

Best Time To Visit

The desert is in stunning full bloom during late March and early April. Unfortunately, that coincides with many colleges' spring breaks, when students are known for heading toward desert climes. Don't visit in the summer unless you will be content avoiding the 120-degree heat by hanging out in shopping malls and movie theaters.

Getting Around

Ideally, Tucson can be navigated best by bicycle. The terrain is basically flat, and, barring any mishaps with cacti, you can get from point A to point B in less than half-an-hour still looking fresh. After all, sweat will evaporate in the dry heat. Remember to pack water bottles. Otherwise, rent a car. Even though Tucson is on the smaller end of the scale of big towns, things are spread out too far for walking. The bottom line is you will need some sort of wheels in order to escape into the desert.

STAY

Hotels

Hotel Congress (311 E. Congress, 622-8848). Built at the turn of the century near the train depot, this wild west hotel has housed many colorful characters, including members of the Jessie James Hole-in-the Wall gang. Popular with twenty-somethings; a hostel is also housed in the main building. $42-60.

Guest Houses

Adobe Rose B&B (940 N. Olsen Ave., 318-4644). A beautifully renovated, lesbian-owned casita near the University of Arizona and Fourth Avenue. Two rooms feature beehive fireplaces and stained-glass windows. Two cottages are also available. Clientele is mixed lesbian and straight. $75.

Bienestar B&B (10490 E. Escalante Rd., 290-1048). Desert hacienda on six acres near Saguaro National Park, with natural foods, solar pool, therapeutic spa, private baths and complimentary horse facilities. Woman-owned. $85-125.

Casa Tierra (11155 W. Calle Pima, 578-3058). Reminiscent of an old Mexico hacienda, Casa Tierra is situated on five acres of remote desert near the Arizona-Sonora Desert Museum and Saguaro National

Park. Private baths, patios and entrances. Full vegetarian breakfast. Very gay friendly. $70-95.

Montecitos (4041 E. Montecito, 327-8586). A comfortable room in a house with a private bath. The cheery owner is active in the community and will be glad to recommend restaurants, hikes and sightseeing spots. Also, enjoy a gazillion complimentary games of pinball in the living room before breakfast. Lesbian-owned. $40.

SEE-DO

In and Around Tucson

Center for Creative Photography (University of Arizona campus near Park Ave. and Speedway Blvd., 621-7968). A contemporary gallery holding America's foremost collection of photographs by master shutterbug Ansel Adams, as well as images by almost every other major photographer of the 20th century.

De Grazia Gallery in the Sun (6300 N. Swan, 299-9191). An ongoing memorial to the late Ted De Grazia, the prolific Tucson artist, whose watercolors of Mexican children won worldwide approval. The unique adobe building was designed by the artist and houses many De Grazia originals.

Desert Voices (791-9662). When scheduling a trip to the area plan to hear one of Tucson's unforgettable gay and lesbian chorus concerts.

Downtown Saturday Nights (Congress, Pennington and Alameda Streets between Granada and Toole, 624-9977). The downtown area, also known as the Arts District, is a lively spot with street entertainment, shops, galleries and cafes that are open late into the night every first and third Saturday of the month.

Garden of Gethsemane (600 W. Congress St. on the west bank of the Santa Cruz River). Artist Felix Lucero hand-sculpted the images of Christ at the Last Supper, on the Cross, and with the Holy Family, in order to have his life spared by the army during World War I.

Sabino Canyon (5900 N. Sabino Canyon Rd., 749-2861). For a tranquil, desert morning jaunt, take the open-air shuttle into this Santa

Catalina Mountains' canyon that is closed to regular traffic, and hike back down the Telephone Line Trail. Moonlight rides three nights per month are available by reservation April through December. Shuttle costs $5.

Thursday Night Art Walks (624-9977). Every week, from September to May, meet at 5:30 p.m. at the Park Inn Santa Rita Hotel (88 E. Broadway) for a free tour of art venues and exhibit openings throughout the Tucson Arts District.

Tohono Chul Park (7366 N. Paseo del Norte, 575-8468). A collection of desert gardens connected by nature trails and regional wildlife. Call ahead for information about its concert series.

Near Tucson

Arizona-Sonora Desert Museum (2021 N. Kinney Rd., 883-2702). Until visiting the living museum's displays of snakes, javelinas, geckos, bobcats, Mexican gray wolves and hummingbirds — all in their natural desert habitats — it is hard to believe the barren land is alive with so many little critters. $9.

Biosphere 2 (30 minutes north of Tucson on Oracle Rd. at mile marker 96.5, 800/828-2462). What could be America's largest terrarium, this hermetically sealed research center showcases an ecological experiment with the goal of better understanding Biosphere 1, which is the earth.

Kitt Peak Observatory (56 miles southwest of Tucson via Routes 86 and 386, 318-8204). The middle of a vast desert — *sans* city lights — is a logical place for a national, astronomical research facility. Was there ever any doubt? Guided tours of the world's largest collection of telescopes cost $2 and last one hour.

Saguaro National Park (773-5158). The newly created national park bookends Tucson on the east and west, each side having a looped road for driving or bicycling. The west side location has picnic areas, campgrounds, and a new visitors' center with a gift shop, museum and auditorium. The east side has a visitors' center, as well.

San Xavier del Bac Mission (located on the Tohono O'odham Indian Reservation southwest of Tucson). Called the "Sistine Chapel of North America" for its frescoes, this mission church still serves the

Native American community for whom it was established in the late 1600s. A Spanish-language service is given on Sundays.

Tubac (45 miles south of Tucson). A former railroad-town-turned-artists' colony. Plan a day to stroll through open studios and historic parks.

KEEP FIT-RECREATION

Arizona Gay Rodeo Association (323-0805).

Cactus Wrens (327-6561). Women's bowling league in the spring and fall.

Frontrunners (326-3555). Meets on Tuesdays, 6 p.m., in front of the Himmel Park Library, at the corner of Speedway and Tucson Streets.

Lichen Hiking Club (622-6229). For all women who long to be within prickling distance of cacti.

EAT

Cast aside expectations of eating many things besides steak or Mexican food. Tortillas are daily bread, and tacquerias are a dime a dozen.

Fine Dining

Tanque Verde Ranch (14301 E. Speedway Blvd., 296-6275). Historic 1868 big sky, chuck wagon-type guest ranch nestled in the Rincon Mountains foothills with fabulous mesquite-grilled New York strip that is barbecued outdoors. $15-35.

Casual Dining

Cafe Magritte (254 E. Congress, 884-8004). Artful fare, spirited atmosphere and an impressive wine list inspire occasional live poetry. $3-14.

Chuy's (356 E. Grant Rd., 624-0636). It's a chain restaurant, and the happy hour margaritas served in salt-rimmed plastic cups might be a turnoff, but indulge anyway. They are the best libation in town. $3-12.

TUCSON

EGGceptions (509 N. Fourth Ave., 791-3060). This is a homemade haven. Chef Cathy is fondly referred to as "Super Mom," what with her late nights baking muffins, cookies and fresh pies. Breakfast is served until 3 p.m. $4-9.

El Charro (311 N. Court, 622-1922). The house specialty is a mouth-watering "carne seca" — sun-dried strips of beef marinated in fresh lime juice, garlic and green chile — and comes in any shape and form: rellenos, enchiladas, tacos, you name it. But brush up on your Spanish before attempting to read the menu. $7-14.

Frank's (3843 E. Pima, 881-2710). Housed in an old purple and yellow gas station, this joint defines the word "greasy." It's as if the place were converted to an eatery in the middle of an oil change. The homemade chorizo is scrumptious, and the no-frills coffee superb. Open for breakfast and lunch only, as well as 9 p.m.-3 a.m. on Friday and Saturday nights. $1.40-6.50.

La Parrilla Suiza (2720 N. Oracle Rd., 624-4300). The traditional cuisine of Mexico is either grilled or cooked over charcoal, then served with handmade corn tortillas and salsas. The green tomato salsa, the garlicky Spanish rice, and the chuleta tacos filled with grilled, boneless pork could become staples of your Tucson diet, if you are not careful. $3-10.

Rincon Market (2513 E. 6th St., 327-6653). The original corner grocery was expanded into a food court that includes a deli, grill, bakery, coffee and salad bars, and a bagel counter. It's a popular meeting place for weekend waffles and grilled breakfasts. $3-6.

Rosa's Mexican Food (1750 E. Fort Lowell Rd., 325-0362). Perfect huevos rancheros — over-easy or fried — covered with a gentle blend of chiles and onions. To die for. $4-10.

Tacqueria Pico de Gallo (2618 S. Sixth Ave., 623-8775). On your return to the airport, stop by this shack for a mouth-watering carne asada burro and an iced horchata — cinnamon milk. After that, it's airplane food. $1-4.

Coffeehouses

Bentley's (1730 Speedway, 795-0338). Nary a table is found without a University of Arizona student indulging in a latté behind a stack of books. Full coffee bar, breakfast of muffins and banana bread, and quiche or healthy sandwiches for lunch. Lesbian-owned. $1-6.

Girlfriends (3540 N. Oracle Rd., Suite 126, 888-GIRL). A one-stop shop for all of your girlie needs. It's a coffee shop, book-card-gift store, dance floor, art gallery and resource center.

Rainbow Planet Coffee House (606 N. Fourth Ave., 620-1770). Tucson's largest selection of specialty coffee drinks. Gay-owned with a hefty clientele of gay men.

The Cup (311 E. Congress, inside Hotel Congress, 798-1618). Hip, eclectic crowd, open late. Lesbian friendly. $2-10.

♪ PLAY-MEET

Dancing

Ain't Nobody's Bizness (2900 E. Broadway, Ste. 118, 318-4838). A nice, upscale lesbian club offering weekly live entertainment of music, comedy, lesbian drag shows and karaoke. Every Tuesday is "Menz Night."

Club Congress (in Hotel Congress, 311 E. Congress, 622-8849). A hot spot for a younger, louder crowd, offering the best in avant-garde and live music. Earplugs are provided free of charge. Mixed; Wednesday is gay and lesbian night.

Hours (3455 E. Grant Rd., 327-3390). This country-western tavern has a friendly neighborhood feel to it. There are free dance lessons every Sunday. Both men and women are welcome.

IBT's (616 N. Fourth Ave., 882-3053). Hang out on the multi-level patio in the back. The historic building and sidewalk entrance give the place an old western "saloon" feel. Mostly men; women are welcome.

The Graduate (23 W. University, 622-9233). Tucson's oldest gay bar is a drinkers' heaven with great prices, and a jukebox with lots of oldies. A new game room features pool tables, darts, pinball and shuffle-board. Primarily a men's bar with women sprinkled throughout.

TUCSON

SHOP

General Shopping

Congress Street and the Downtown Arts District are especially good areas to browse. One-of-a-kind items can also be found in artsy boutiques on Fourth Avenue, between Second and Ninth Streets. The Mexican border town of Nogales, 65 miles south of Tucson, attracts hard-core bargain hunters. Look for colorful serapes, terra cotta pots, tin-work mirrors and discounted liquor. The **Old Town Artisans** complex (186 N. Meyer Ave., 623-6024) brings together a fine group of purveyors of southwestern wares. Also, try **Rainbow Moods** (3532 E. Grant Rd., 326-9643). Smudge-stick central, this woman-owned, metaphysical, Native American store has everything for a woman's spiritual quest: crystals, oils, books and kachina dolls.

Food Markets

Food Conspiracy Coop (412 N. Fourth Ave., 624-4821). Where the hip and healthful vegetarians shop; located on the main shopping strip across from Antigone bookstore.

Pride Shopping

Tucson Trunk (5606 S. River Road, 529-8309). Pride gifts, outrageous cards.

Bookstores

Antigone Books (411 N. Fourth Ave., 792-3715). A spacious and welcoming hot spot. What can't be found elsewhere in women's music can be found here, as well as books, jewelry, calendars and children's books.

Girlfriends Coffeehouse (3540 N. Oracle Rd., Suite 126, 888-GIRL, www.girlscafe.com). A good collection of lesbian titles, cards and trinkets.

🦋 KIDS' STUFF

Colossal Cave (20 miles southeast of Tucson on Old Spanish Trail, 647-7275). One of the largest dry caverns, and its end has yet to be discovered. Legend has it that a buried treasure is still deep inside the cave, leftover from bandits one hundred years ago.

Ice Cream. Baskin-Robbins has 14 locations. Take advantage. Remember it *is* the desert.

Old Tucson Studios (201 S. Kinney Rd., 883-0100). Since the 1939 filming of the appropriately named movie *"Arizona,"* more than 200 movies, commercials and documentaries have emerged from this desert Hollywood-esque studio. A major fire closed the facility in 1995, and it was subsequently re-vamped with an additional theme park.

Tombstone (75 miles southeast of Tucson). Known as "the town that's too tough to die," Tombstone was a notorious outlaw hangout back in its heyday. Today, you can visit the OK Corral, Boothill Graveyard and the Court House Museum.

Yozeum (2900 N. Country Club, 322-0100). This Yo-yo museum displays the Duncan family yo-yo collection, as well as the Playmaxx yo-yo factory.

☀ SPIRITUAL

Christian Science Group (371-1102). Monthly outreach meeting for gays and lesbians in Arizona.

Cornerstone Fellowship (2902 N. Geronimo, 622-4626). Gay friendly Evangelical Church with HIV-AIDS ministry luncheon the first and third Sunday of each month, 1:30 p.m.

Dignity Tucson (4005 N. Stone Ave., 744-3400). Lesbian, gay and bisexual Catholics.

Gay and Lesbian Spirituality Group (323-7943). Meets in the Hills Episcopal Church every first and third Monday night at 7:30 p.m.

Living Waters Family Center (at the MCC Church, 3269 N. Mountain, 795-7266). Worship services are on Mondays at 5 p.m.

TUCSON

RESOURCES

General Information

Tucson Visitor's Bureau (130 S. Scott Ave., 888/2-TUCSON).

Bisexual, Gay and Lesbian Association (621-7585). Meets every other Thursday at 5 p.m. on campus.

Forty and Better Women's Group (623-6040). Breakfast meetings every second Saturday at 9 a.m. for lesbians over forty.

Lambda Car Club (318-0540). A social organization for gay men and lesbians who share interest in those old jalopies.

Lesbian Cancer Project (738 N. Fifth Ave, 884-7810).

Lesbian Support Group (422 N. Fourth Ave., 624-1779). Meets the second and fourth Wednesdays of each month, 7-8:30 p.m. at Wingspan.

Lesbianas Latinas de Tucson (624-1779). Meets every first and third Tuesday of the month, at Wingspan, 5:30-7 p.m.

Shanti Foundation (300 E. Sixth St., 622-7107). The all-important AIDS center.

T-Squares (2902 N. Geronimo, 762-9135). Lesbian and gay square dance club meets every Tuesday night, 6:30-9 p.m. at the Cornerstone Fellowship Social Hall.

Wingspan Community Center (422 N. Fourth Ave., 624-1779). The gay and lesbian community center's lending library will loan books to tourists.

Media

Rubyfruit Journal (517 E. Gay St., 888-5371). An exclusively lesbian, monthly publication. Can be purchased at Girlfriends or Antigone.

The Observer (622-7176, bonzo.com/observer). Weekly Tucson gay and lesbian newspaper, with the emphasis on gay men.

Transformer (864-7682). Southern Arizona's monthly networking resource.

Tucson Weekly (792-3630, www.tucsonweekly.com). The place to look for weekly events' listings.

Index

a

A Different Bite Cafe............93
A Different Drummer............64
A Different Light Bookstore
    Los Angeles............59
    New York............96
    San Francisco............111
Adobe Rose B&B............207
Advocate............162
African-American Lesbian and Gay Alliance............14
Afrocentric Bookstore............46
Ain't Nobody's Bizness............212
Alameda Lesbian Potluck Society............113
Alexandria II Bookstore............59
ALPS, Associated Lesbians of Puget Sound............217
Alternative Cards and Gifts............84
Amazon Bookstore............70
Amethyst............14
Angelica Kitchen............92
Ann Sathers Restaurant............42
Annapurna Inn............175
Antigone Books............213
Apple Valley B&B............155
Area 52............21
ARF............196
Audrey Lorde Lesbian Health Clinic............218
Austin Chronicle............24
Austin Latino Lesbian and Gay Organization............24
Austin Motel............17

b

Bailey/Coy Books............123
Bar d'O............94
Bay Area Reporter............114
Bay Times............114
Bay Windows............36
Bayou Women's Tennis Club............80
Bed & Breakfast on the Park............99
Bee Charmer Inn............165
Bella Luna............32
Berlin............44
Bernal Books............111
Beyond the Closet Bookstore............123
Beyond Words Books............218
Bienstar B&B............218
Big Chicks............44
Bisexual Network of Austin............24
Black Lesbian Support Group............136
Black Lines............49

Blade ... 61
Bloomsbury Books ... 170
Blue Moon Coffee Cafe ... 70
Blue Wave ... 32
Boadecia's ... 112
Bon Vivant ... 136
Bonaventure ... 7
Book Shop of the Minnesota Women's Press ... 72
Book Woman ... 16
Bookstar ... 84
Boston Bed & Breakfast Associates ... 219
Bradford Gardens Inn ... 185
Breakaway Cycling Group ... 19
Brick Hut ... 108
Broadway Market ... 116
Butch-Femme Society ... 98
By the Book ... 62
Bywater B&B ... 77

C

Cactus Wrens ... 210
Cafe Berlin ... 133
Cafe Flore ... 108
Cafe Luna ... 133
Cafe Wyrd ... 70
Café Crudité ... 190
Café du Monde ... 76
Café Marigny ... 82
Cahoots Coffee Bar ... 71
Cambridge Bed and Muffin ... 29
Cambridge Women's Center ... 36
Capitol Hill Inn ... 117
Carry Nation ... 99
Casa Laguna Inn ... 63
Celebration Books ... 170
Centre Street Cafe ... 32
Centrum Cultural Center ... 176
Charis Books and More ... 12
Charlene's ... 78
Check'er Inn Resort ... 186
Chelsea Piers Sports Complex ... 91
Chelsea Pines Inn ... 89
Chicago Area Gay and Lesbian Chamber of Commerce ... 48
Chiltern Mountain Club ... 31
Chrysalis Women's Health Center ... 73
Circles ... 5
Clique ... 98
Clit Club ... 94
Club 3772 ... 57
Club Cafe ... 33
Club Casanova ... 94
Club Intimus ... 44

Club Metro	71
Club Q	109
Coffeehouse for Women with HIV/AIDS	133
Connection	51
Cornerstone Community Center	24
Cornstalk Hotel	221
Cottage, Laguna Beach	221
Country Comfort B&B	53
Cousins	42
Crazy Nanny's	94
Creative Loafing	14
Crescent Moon	9
Cubbyhole	94

d

Dana's After Dark	200
De Colores	162
Deaf Gay and Lesbian Center	113
Desert Business Association	171
Desert Daily Guide	171
Desert Palms Inn	165
Desert Sun	171
Desert Voices	208
Dexter's Inn	186
Different Spokes	106
Donna's	83
DP Poolside Bar	169
Drama Club	200
Dusty Miller Inn	186
Dyke Hackers	106
Dykespeak	111

e

East Side Cafe	20
East Village B&B	90
El Sol y La Luna	16
Elliott Bay Bookstore	123
ETC	14
Everywoman's Center	162

f

fab!	61
Fairbanks Inn	186
Faster Pussycat	109
Faubourg-Marigny Bookstore	84
Feelings Café	81
Flying Biscuit Cafe	6
Focus Point	74
Food for Thought Books	161
Footsteps Theatre	40
Fuel	58
Full Circle Books	201

g

G-Spot	24
Gabriel's	186
Gaia's Getaway	175
Galaxy	54
Galisteo News	194
Gay 90s	67
Gay and Lesbian Center, Atlanta	223
Gay and Lesbian Community Center of Colorado	152
Gay and Lesbian Community Center of Los Angeles	223
Gay and Lesbian Community Services Center of Long Beach	223
Gay and Lesbian International Film Festival	25
Georgia O'Keefe Museum	196
Gerber-Hart Gay and Lesbian Library Archives	48
Ginger's Guest House	175
Girl Bar	33
Girl Guide	61
Girlfriends	36
Girls in the Night	11
Glad Day Books	35
Good Vibrations	110
Gull Walk Inn	186

h

Halle's	186
Henrietta Hudson	94
Henrietta's	99
Her/She Bar	94
Heritage House	186
Hilltop House	53
Hotel Amsterdam	67
Hours	1
House O' Chicks	104
Hummingbird Ranch	195
Hung Jury	134
Hungry Mind Bookstore	72
HX for Her	98

i

IBT's	212
Impact	85
IN Newsweekly	36
Inn of the Turquoise Bear	195
Innamorata B&B	155

j

Josie's Cabaret and Juice Joint	107
Julia's in Wallingford	120
Juliana Hotel	103
Julie's	95
June L. Mazer Lesbian Archives	54

Just For You Bakery and Cafe 109

k
Kalorama Guest House............................. 129
Kid Mohair... 122
Kindred Hearts Women's Center 48
Kitty Glitter 94
Koko Bar... 99

l
LA Weekly... 61
La Covina 70
Lady Golf.. 169
Lady Jane's Inn..................................... 186
Lambda Book Report 137
Lambda Rising bookstore............................ 227
Lammas Women's Books & More..................... 135
Las Buenas Amigas 98
Latina Lesbian Organization........................... 24
Lavender Rose 187
Le Ms.. 38
Lesbian and Gay Community Center, New Orleans......... 227
Lesbian and Gay Community Services Center, New York 227
Lesbian Clinic 60
Lesbian Herstory Archives 88
Lesbian News....................................... 61
Lesbian Resource Center, Seattle 227
Lesbianas Latinas de Tucson......................... 215
LesboEXPO 171
LGNY 98
Little Frida's.. 51
Little River Farm 155
Lizzie's 175
Los Angeles Asian Pacific Islander Sisters................ 61
LRC News... 125

m
Magnolia Place B&B................................. 39
Mama Bears 112
Manhattan B&B Reservation Center..................... 89
May Day Cafe...................................... 70
Mentone B&B 77
Meow Mix 94
Mercury Bar-Esmé 33
Metro Arts Entertainment Weekly...................... 137
Mews... 189
Michelle's XXX 58
Minnesota Women's Press............................ 72
Modern Times...................................... 68
Montecitos.. 208
Moore Magic....................................... 85
Moors Motel 185

Motherwear 161
Mountain Moving Coffeehouse for Womyn and Children 43
Ms. C's 151
Muffdive 109

n

Nabisco-Dinah Shore LPGA 163
Nan's Bed & Breakfast 67
National Museum of Women in the Arts 131
New City 49
New Words Bookstore 35
Nightlines 49
Nora's 132
Northampton Area Lesbian and Gay Business Guild 162
NYC Apartment Swap Service 89

o

off our backs 137
Offbeat 86
Old Arizona Cafe 70
Old Arizona Studio 68
Old Red Schoolhouse and Lesbian Towers 156
Old Town B&B 40
One Hot Spot 100
Open Sky 195
Optimist 162
Oscar Wilde Memorial Books 96
Osento 105
Otherside 11
Our Hideaway 159
Out Front 21
Out! 2
Outlines 49
Outwrite 12
Over

p

Palm Springs Athletic Club 167
Paris Dance 44
Park Lane Guest House 16
Pauline's 42
Pearl Street Nightclub 159
Pearl's Booksellers 62
Peninsula Daily News 181
People Like Us Books 230
Phase One 134
Phoenix Rising Bookstore 230
Pied Piper Lounge 190
Pink Zone 122
Plums B&B 187
Pop Stop 130
Port Townsend Women's Center 230

Postmark New Orleans. 84
Prairie Moon 46
Pride Agenda 46
Pride and Joy 160
Pride's of Provincetown 191
Provincetown Advocate 192
Provincetown Banner 192
Provincetown magazine 192

q

Q Monthly 74
Q San Francisco. 114
Quatrefoil Library 74
Que Sera. 62
Quest 152

r

Railyard Bookstore 202
Rainbow Clinic 113
Ravenscroft Inn. 175
Ravenwood Guest House. 187
Recovering Hearts Bookstore. 191
Red & Black Books 123
Red Dora's Bearded Lady Cafe 108
Revolution 11
Rising Cafe 88
Rose Acre 187
Rosebud Espresso and Bistro 121
Rosewalk House 77
Ruby's Cafe 70
Rubyfruit Bar and Grill. 93
Rubyfruit Journal. 215
Rubyfruit Jungle 76
Rumors 5

s

Sanctuary 99
SapphFire 24
Sappho Rainbow. 58
Sappho-nics 157
Seattle Bisexual Women's Network 125
Seattle Gay News 125
Seattle Weekly 125
She-Bang 95
Shescape 95
Sirens 151
Sisterspace Books 135
Sojourner 36
Southern Voice 14
Spectrum Disco. 100
Stonewall Center. 162
Susie's Mopeds. 177

t

Tabard Inn B&B 129
Team D.C. Velo 132
Texas Triangle 24
The Ark 202
The Book Garden 152
The Bottom Line 171
The Easy 120
The Elle 151
The Enclave 165
The Graduate 212
The Huntress 57
The Jungle 33
The Leader 146
The Lesbian Calendar 162
The Lesbian Connection 66
The Names Project 105
The Observer 215
The Old House 67
The Palms 57
The San Antonio Marquise 24
The Weekly Guide 86
Third Wave Feminist Bookstore 161
This Week In Texas 25
Threadgills 21
Three Lives 96
Timberline 121
Time Out New York 98
Tin Roof B&B 156
Tomboy 42
Townhouse 29
Toys in Babeland 122
Transformer 215
Tri Women 41
Triangle Inn 195
Trident Booksellers and Cafe 148
Trumpets 132
Tucker Inn 187
Tucson Weekly 215
Twin Peaks Tavern 110

u

U-Mass Lambda Line 162
UltraViolet 125
Unique of Denver 152

v

Val 21 108
Van Go's Ear 57
Venture Out 158
Venus magazine 14

Newcomer's Handbooks™

THE ORIGINAL, ALWAYS UPDATED, ABSOLUTELY INVALUABLE GUIDES FOR PEOPLE *MOVING* TO A CITY!

Find out about neigborhoods, apartment hunting, money matters, deposits/leases, getting settled, helpful services, shopping for the home, places of worship, belonging, sports/recreation, vounteering, green space, transportation, temporary lodgings and useful telephone numbers!

	# COPIES		TOTAL
Newcomer's Handbook™ for Atlanta	_____	x $13.95	$_____
Newcomer's Handbook™ for Boston	_____	x $13.95	$_____
Newcomer's Handbook™ for Chicago	_____	x $12.95	$_____
Newcomer's Handbook™ for Los Angeles	_____	x $12.95	$_____
Newcomer's Handbook™ for Minneapolis-St. Paul	_____	x $14.95	$_____
Newcomer's Handbook™ for New York City	_____	x $17.95	$_____
Newcomer's Handbook™ for San Francisco	_____	x $13.95	$_____
Newcomer's Handbook™ for Washington D.C.	_____	x $13.95	$_____

SUBTOTAL $_____

TAX (*IL residents add 8.75% sales tax*) $_____

POSTAGE & HANDLING (*$4.00 first book, $.75 each add'l*) $_____

TOTAL $_____

SHIP TO:

Name _____

Title _____

Company _____

Address _____

City _____ State _____ Zip _____

Phone Number (___) _____

FIRST BOOKS

Send this order form and a check or money order payable to: First Books, Inc.

First Books, Inc., Mail Order Department
P.O. Box 578147, Chicago, IL 60657
773-276-5911

Allow 2-3 weeks for delivery

Victorian B&B 29
Victorian Townhouse 29
Viktor/Viktoria 63
Vixen. 184
Vulva Riot 68

W X Y Z

Walnut Cafe 141
Wander Women 132
Washington Blade. 137
We're Everywhere. 46
Weird Sisters. 150
West Berkeley Women's Books 112
White Wind Inn 187
Wild Side West 110
Wilderness Women. 106
Wildrose Tavern 120
Wiminfest 203
Windamar House 187
Windy City Times 49
Winged One 72
Wingspan Community Center. 215
Witches Closet 84
Woman Made Gallery 46
Woman Wild Treasures by Women 46
Woman's Monthly 137
Women About. 92
Women and Their Work 18
Women in the Wilderness. 69
Women on Two Wheels 146
Women Unlimited Magazine. 162
Women Who Run With Women 56
Women's Building. 106
Women's Healthy Pages. 86
Women's Heritage Trail 29
Women's Music Collective 86
Women's Outdoor Club. 146
Women's Outdoor Network. 9
Women's Philharmonic. 106
Women's Place Resource Center. 48
Women's Program of Howard Brown Health Center 48
Women's Training Center. 107
Women's Voices. 203
Women's Wednesday Night Group. 202
Women's Works 74
Womyn of Color 86
Womyn of Wheels. 119
Woodswomen. 69
Word Is Out Women's Bookstore 149
Yard of Ale 141
ZAMI 14